Excerpts From *Black Watch Diary, A Sequel*

The spirit of all-weather Jet-Fighter Interceptor Airmen flying the air defense mission:

We Can Beat Any Man
From Any Land
At Any Game
That He Can Name
For Any Amount
That He Can Count

When The Ducks Walk at Goose, We Fly!

Scramble Inn Plaque:

There is a place named Scramble Inn
That the boys of 59th have settled in,
Where fun and frolic always win.
A grin under the wondrous warmth of a little gin.
Of course, the need of this nightly din
Finds its purpose in practices many call sin.
But, whatever the world would judge
To label this cellar retreat, with grudge,
It's the one place on Goose where a guy can let loose.

"Tower, this is Jellybean Leader with a flight of two Jellybeans checking the runway to see if it is still straight before we come in to land." Then to the wingman, "OK Jellybean Flight, kick in the afterburner and dust off the runway!"

---

5 February 1955:
At 10 p.m., Dave White with RO Burt Tillet, returned from his Scramble Sortie and decided to buzz the Saturday night Scramble Inn party. At about 90 feet, he struck a 100-foot-high unlighted radio tower...

What Others Are Saying About *Black Watch Diary*

Mike Goodman, Bike Shop Owner, Aviation History Buff, Atlanta, GA
"Colonel Batchelder's book is an insight into the history of that time. It gives one an inside look at both the dangerous and mundane life of a bunch of young, raucous flyers that 'stood the wall' for us during the Cold War. I thoroughly enjoyed the read."

Stefanie Sage, Avid Reader, Peoria, IL
"An intriguing insight into the world of a 'fly-boy.' The individual isolation coupled with unique camaraderie gave me cause to reflect upon the immense personal sacrifices that our military men made and continue to make for the freedom we so often take for granted. The account made me smile and shudder, all the while pondering the world as it once was while contrasting it to the world in which we now live."

Donald R. Reed, Attorney, Sierra Madre, CA
"Just received *Black Watch Diary* and had to leaf through it before doing anything else. I am so impressed I would like to order two more copies for our daughters. The pictures of the F-94Bs are impressive. We were flying those when the F-89C was grounded becuase their wings kept breaking."

T. Wayne Evans, Columbia, TN
"Just got the book and couldn't put it down. It is a pleasure to hear from someone who has walked the frozen tundra of the Goose. I was an enlisted man and crew chief of an F-89 and the B-25 'Hangar Queen'."

Jim Wiggins, Youngstown, FL
"I was a crew chief on the F-94C. When I arrived at Goose, we didn't even have alert hangars."

Colonel Theodore R. Legako, USAF, Retired, Stillwater, OK
"Received your book yesterday and read most of it immediatley. It certainly brought back some old memories of Goose. It was the most interesting year of my life."

Richard P. Winterberg, Southern Pines, NC
"Building the Scramble Inn in the basement of the barracks was a highlight. Goose Bay was the highlight of my life and I've told the stories a million times."

Don Harvey, Englewood, FL
"I enjoyed your *Black Watch Diary*. Our duty at Hamilton AFB, CA was not so austere but riddled with aircraft accidents and unusual incidents...really an experience for naive young officers first out of training. My roommate and his pilot were killed in an F-94B on a clear, dark and moonless night when they flew into the water after being waved off to give priority to a scramble flight."

Gailen Rosenberg, Dunwoody, GA
"The mission to protect America from attack, under the most brutal conditions that Mother Nature can dish out was truly amazing...I am grateful for reading about all of the men of the Black Watch and want to thank each one."

Jackie Goldammer, Consultant, Atlanta, GA
"For Lt. Colonel Batchelder to share these words now, with stories from fellow airmen, families and friends, bestows honor on all who served. Well done!"

Black Watch Diary

A Sequel

Life Is A Tragedy For Those Who Feel, And A Comedy For Those Who Think

–Horace Walpole
(1717-1797)

Josh Batchelder
Lt. Colonel USAF (RET.)

Second Edition
Copyright © 2009 Josh Batchelder

For additional information contact:
Josh Batchelder
P.O. Box 450525, Atlanta, GA 31145-0525
Phone 770.621.9000
joshbatchelder@bellsouth.net

ISBN: 978-1-934216-56-9

To purchase additional copies of *Black Watch Diary...a Sequel*, please visit:
www.blackwatchdiary.com

Or contact the publisher:
United Writers Press
Asheville, N.C.
www.unitedwriterspress.com

Cover and interior photographs of aircraft were provided by and are printed with the permission of The National Museum of the U.S. Air Force.

Acknowledgments

Audrey Dixon, of Dixon's Word Processing, faithfully struggled to read my carefree handwritten script, and she helped me by patiently listening to my search for better ways to express messages. She made valuable suggestions that freed me to move on to the next series of dilemmas. My loving sister, Nancy Sephton, valiantly and kindly suggested more punctuating of my punctuation. I had excess commas, quotation marks, and lengthy sentences. Special thanks to Betty Ann Sage, my very social bride. She endured my frequent non-social retreats to my "cave" to focus on writing. Vally Sharpe and Jan Lowe of United Writers Press allowed me to barge in and passionately tell them about my youthful past experiences. Noel Griese of Anvil Press was my experienced guide to the publishing world. The National U.S. Air Force Museum at Wright Patterson AFB, Ohio, graciously forwarded a CD containing photographs of the aircraft I flew in during the nineteen fifties.

Many 59th members and others from Air Defense units came forward with heartfelt stories and pictures of their tours of duty at Goose and elsewhere. Widows of our airmen shared their fond memories. It soon became clear that a second edition would add interesting and humorous memories that would enrich my story of life on the Goose. This second edition honors more members; the chapter notes, and Epilogue/Legacy expansions capture many of their stories, aviation achievements, and civilian community contributions.

Especially notable was a letter from Colonel Robert E. Fritsch's widow, Debbie. Bob, at age 25, as he was departing Goose (1953) composed a beautiful poem about flying. It captured the Goose experience for the 59th airmen. She wrote me about her oldest son Lt. Colonel Robert, Jr., an F-16 pilot with the Wisconsin Air National Guard. After she bought copies of the *Black Watch Diary* for herself and Robert, her daughter and other two sons demanded their personally autographed copies. Be sure to savor Bob's poem on pages 78-79.

Black Watch Diary

John "JJ" Johnston from Horse Shoe Bay, Texas supplied many pictures and comments. I remember well his always ready and enduring smile. Now, almost daily I receive humorous, political and other subject e-mails. "JJ" leads the charge to remind us all of what has made America exceptional. He resists the socialist movements that foster group thinking over individual freedoms.

My pilot Al Kramer, and his wife Barbara, loaned me their collection of slides from the Goose Tour. Barbara also wrote me a rich description of Al's long Air Force career assignments and subsequent civilian aviation work. Their Air Force family life would be the envy of many. In 1964 Barbara stayed in Saigon for four months while Al was on assignment. You will enjoy reading about their family life in Alaska and elsewhere. Her story is a memoir worth telling.

Bob Russell, Columbia, S.C., sent me his memoir, *Touching the Face of God*. His chapter about his experience at Goose captures the scenery and remote sub-arctic flying hazards of adverse weather.

Al Perry was a principal founder of the "world famous" Scramble Inn. He sent me the saga of how squadron officers playfully responded to being banned from the Base Officers Club. Perry said, "Ken Lengfield was a faithful roommate and fellow collaborator…other early volunteers preparing the Scramble Inn playground' were Jim Rawlings, Lee Grude, Avery Miller and Glen Paulk."

Squadron CO, Fergus "Fergie" Fay and his wife Lesla, died last year within six months of each other. Their daughter, Marilyn Fay-Backen, wrote to me, and included their obituaries. They covered Fergie's military life beginning as WWII Squadron CO and continued through the Cold War, Korean, and Vietnam Wars. Following active duty, he worked on the F-100, B-70, B-1B and space shuttle. Lesla, like many highly relevant military spouses, made Fergie's achievements possible. She also acted as "Mother Superior" to their children and grandchildren. Their stories deserve to be told.

Don Rogers mailed me the 7-page 2001 Reunion stories with more details about the construction and décor of the Scramble Inn. He lived it. After its completion, I arrived to enjoy it. Don also added to my 59th library. He supplied many facts about the 59th and highlighted some of the significant aviation achievements of our members, such as altitude and speed records in the F-104

Josh Batchelder

Starfighter, Captina Walter Irwin achieved a speed of 1,404 mph in 1958. Also, in the Starfighter, Major "Scrappy" Johnson climbed to an altitude of 91,249 feet.

Don Harvey, Englewood, Florida, wrote to me about the hazardous weather of West Coast flying at Hamilton AFB, California that contributed to flight accidents.

Another reader, Donald R. Reed, Attorney, Sierra Madre, California wrote to me about his recollection of the Northrop F89C wings breaking apart during the days when he was flying the F94B.

Dave White, pilot, e-mailed his recollection of three aircraft accidents. Included were pictures and observations of his near fatal accident when one dark night he had an airborne brush with a hundred foot unlighted radio tower. Rex Winchell, Allison Service Representative (aircraft engines), filled me in with his memories of comrades and events of ground personnel who supported our air defense mission.

Naturally, I had to seek and find an appropriate English woman with Royal Navy experience to review my first edition and make suggestions toward enhancing the 2nd edition. Jackie Goldammer (Radio Operator) had unique knowledge of WWII and the Cold War period, and consequent ability to appreciate the Continental and North American mindset.

Many thanks to all.

Dedication

This memoir is dedicated to all my friends and comrades who died too soon serving our country's freedoms, especially to Bill Taylor, pilot and his Radar Observer (RO), Phil Gereau; they joined me at Paine AFB, Washington, following our Goose Air Base tour. One month before I separated to complete my college education and fly with the National Guard, they hit Mt. Diablo due to a combination of adverse weather and controller clearance mistakes.

Again, because of weather, pilot Curt Stegner and RO Al Culpepper collided with fellow pilot Don Leonard and RO John Shepard on Lake Melville ice. Curt had just thirteen days of marriage with his beautiful sweetheart Canadian bride, Winnie, before fate ended their bright future.

And to pilot Lt. Clark whose demise occured following a flame-out and crash landing and RO Gaddess who successfully ejected before the crash.

Colonel Robert E. Fritsch, Goose tour 1952-53, is an example of the talent and service of 59th members both at Goose and after Goose in the Air Force and civilian life. See pages 78-79 for his poem written while at Goose, and the Epilogue/Legacy chapter for excerpts from his obituary.

Contents

Acknowledgments		v
Dedication		viii
Preface		xi
One	Assignment Labrador: Black Watch Squadron	1
Two	Northwest to Goose Airbase	10
Three	When The Ducks Walk, We Fly!	13
Four	The Scramble Inn	18
Five	Pinetree Ground Control	29
Six	Vell, Iss You From Missouri?	33
Seven	Scramble, Crash, and Burn	35
Eight	Chasing Flying Saucers	37
Nine	Flame-Out! Angels Twelve	39
Ten	The Scorpions Are Coming	41
Eleven	A Bun In The Oven	44
Twelve	The Little Theatre	50
Thirteen	The Bob Hope Show	54
Fourteen	"You No Survive, You Dead"	58
Fifteen	Be A Panther, Not a Tiger	61
Sixteen	Arctic Doldrums	68
Seventeen	Escaping Goose	71
Eighteen	FIGMO, Time To Go	75
Epiloque/Legacy		81
Glossary		86
International Phonetic Alphabet		88
Notes		89

Newfoundland and Labrador

Preface

   BLACK WATCH DIARY is a true story of the cocky young fly-boys of the U.S. Air Force 59th all-weather jet fighter-interceptor squadron (FIS). Their 1950s and 60s Cold War mission was defending Canada and the U.S. from Soviet nuclear bombers coming over the short arctic routes. Successful 1949 atomic tests by the Soviets convinced analysts that thousands of nuclear weapons could soon become the first direct threat to the Continental U.S. and Canadian territories. The rush was on to build a network of land-based, long-range radar stations across Alaska, Canada and Greenland; then position squadrons of all-weather airborne radar-equipped jet interceptors. In October, 1952, the 59th FIS was moved from Otis Air Force Base Massachussets, to Goose Bay, Labrador, Canada. Two months later, to counter the frequent Russian aircraft incursions into the Greenland territory, the Pentagon secretly dispatched a flight of four 59th aircraft and crews to the new Greenland, Thule Airbase. Military and U.S. civilian fears created an atmosphere similar to our post 9/11 mindset. Rapid improvements in jet aircraft, ground and airborne radar systems took place.

   The WWII air defense of England had demonstrated the value of good ground and airborne radars. For example, the Northrop P-61 "Black Widow" night fighter aircraft over England shot down many German aircraft and "buzz" bombs headed for London.

   The 59th "tigers" often had to fly in heavy snow, ice, fierce winds, and sub-zero temperatures. They earned their motto: "When the ducks walk at Goose, we fly!" Like firemen, when the scramble alarm sounded, pilots and their radar observers (RO's) would climb ladders to their cockpits. As their jet engines began turning, they would fasten their seat belts and shoulder harnesses; and then don their helmets and oxygen masks. Huge alert hangar doors would snap up and allow quick taxi to the active runway.[1] Igniting their afterburners they would blast off to climb to the altitude and ground controllers directed heading to intercept the *bandit* (enemy aircraft) or *bogey* (unknown or friendly aircraft) breaching the CADIZ (Canadian Air Defense Identification Zone). On red alert, the standard was three (3) minutes from alarm to airborne.

   When the interceptor's airborne radar picked up the bandit or bogey, the RO (Radar Observer) would then assume control. He would direct the pilot to intercept the target aircraft by giving commands to climb, descend, turn port (left) or starboard (right), increase speed or throttle back. Once within close visual range, the aircrew would radio the bogey's aircraft type and tail number to GCI (Ground Control Intercept). At night, with the interceptor's exterior lights off, the pilot would fly close-in alongside the bogey. The RO would then shine his Aldous lamp (spotlight) on the bogey's tail and read the number to GCI.

Many of the events recounted through the eyes of Lt. Batchelder are typical of remote base duty. Some are not. For example, chasing flying saucers and Bob Hope's Christmas Show. These rambunctious young flight crews boredom often resulted in humorous situations and sometimes very risky behavior. When air crews were not on alert duty their days were filled with drinking, swearing, dancing, games, and reading. During Josh Batchelder's one year tour, flying as Radar Observer, he witnessed a succession of five squadron commanders' attempts to stem the tide of eleven aircraft accidents. Tragedy and humor abounded.

While the winnings and losses at *Indian Dice*, poker, and other card table games may appear small, they are not. For example, considering inflation averaging four percent the last fifty-four years, a dollar won or lost, then, would have doubled every eighteen years. For example, during 1954, an $8.50 winning would be equivalent to $68.00 today (doubling three times).

Labrador's territory is covered with an abundance of rivers, lakes, and rugged hilly terrain (see Labrador map). Extreme and changing weather conditions often prevail. Triple-A Auto Guide says it all: "There are two ways to access Happy Valley and Goose Air Base, by air or boat." Population: Labrador Caribou 500,000.[2] Native Aborigine Indians and hardy settlers about 1,000; 8,000 other civilians were involved with maintaining the Air Base.

Besides serving air defense operations and SAC (Strategic Air Command) missions, Goose was a vital refueling and emergency Air Base. It served the military and civilian transatlantic and polar flights. As a sub-arctic region, it was about one hundred miles south of the tree-line. Visitors flying into Goose, next to Happy Valley, are most likely those seeking the thrills of great game fishing or hunting.

Today, Goose is a valuable training facility for NATO nations due to its sub-arctic climate, long runways, and support services.

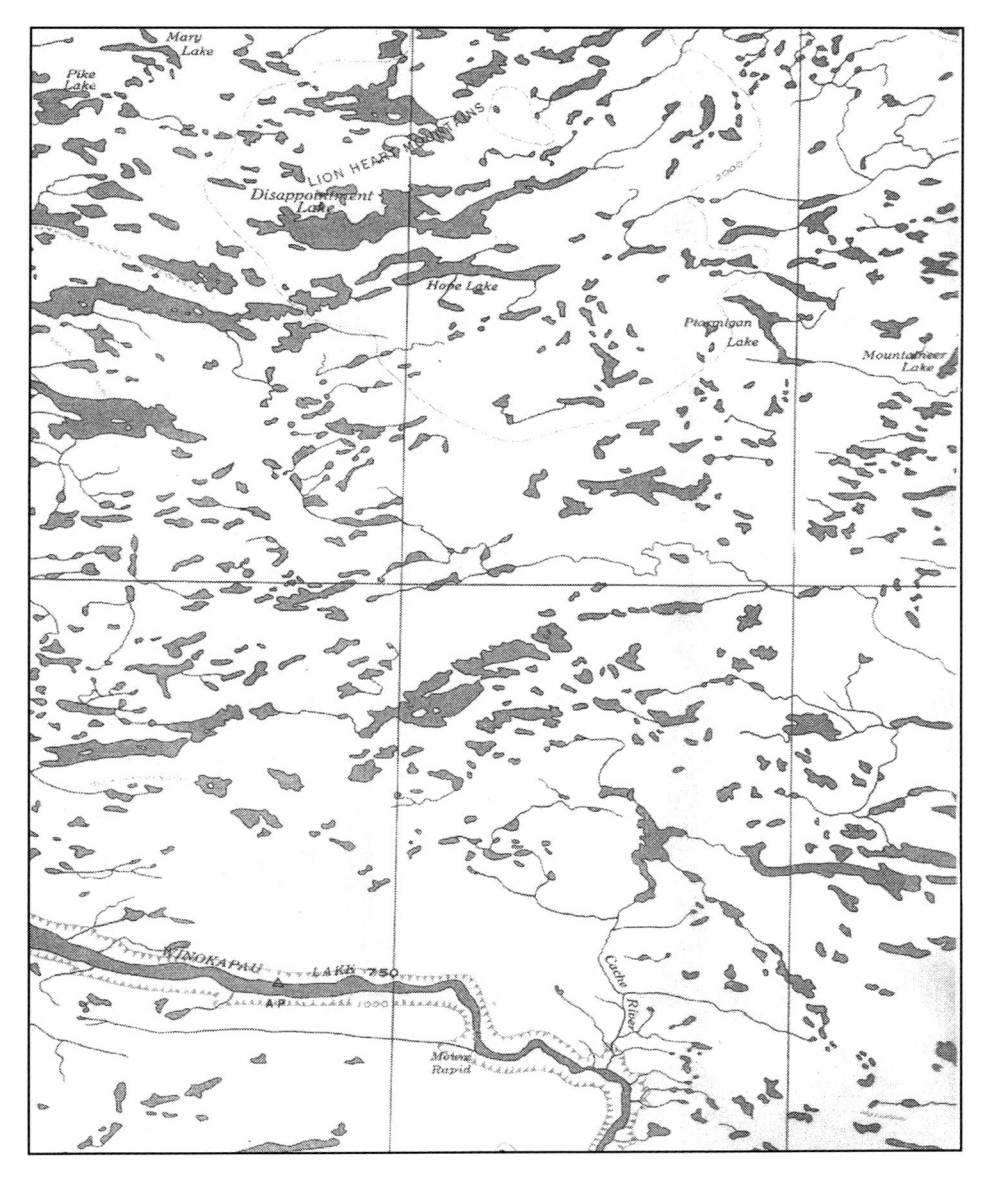

An Abundance of Rivers and Lakes

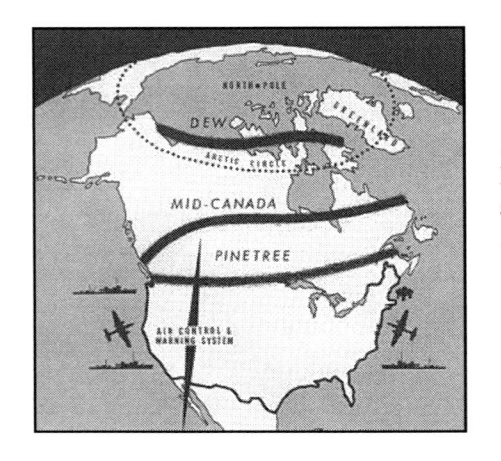

Map Showing the "Dew Line" or Distant Early Warning Line. The Dew Line was a system of radar stations in the far nothern Arctic regions of Canada. It was set up to detect incoming Soviet bombers during the Cold War.

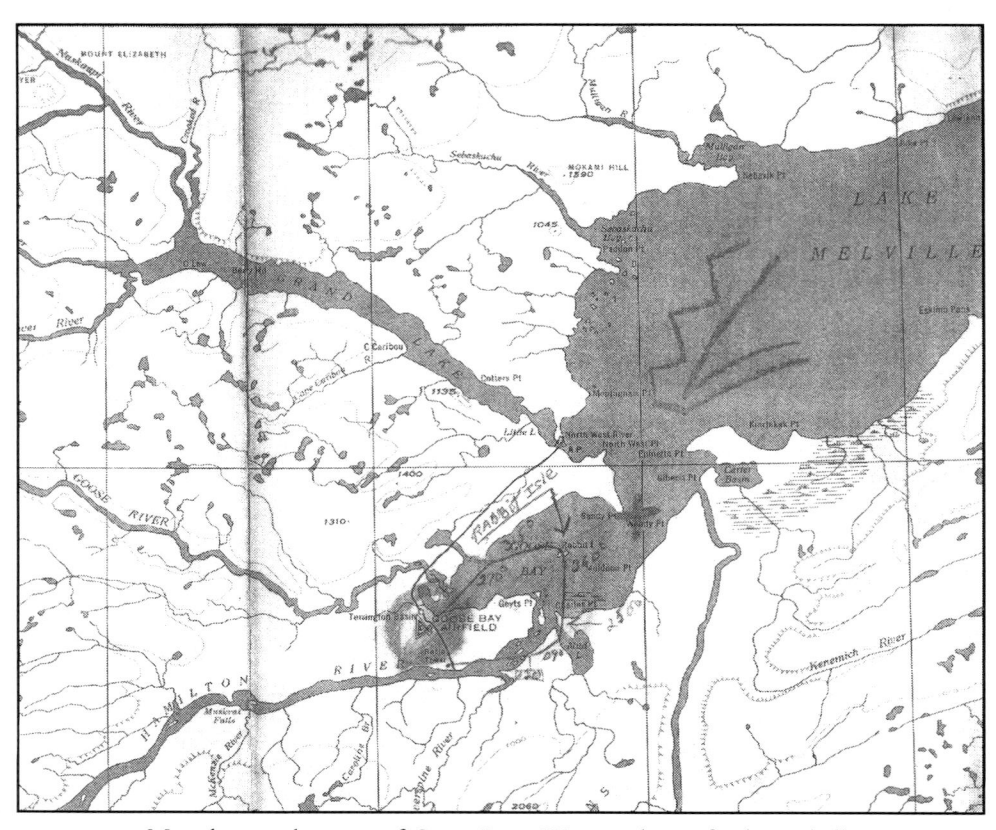

Map showing location of Goose Bay - Western shore of Lake Melville

One

Assignment Labrador
Black Watch Squadron

28 April 1954: Westover Air Force Base, Mass, 1230 hours

We're taking off, wheels up, and climbing to altitude. Within minutes we flew over my hometown, Sudbury, Massachusetts. I'm headed to sub-arctic Goose Air Base, Labrador, Canada. It's an air defense base on the western tip of Lake Melville.

For me, 2nd Lt. Josh Batchelder, life hasn't been dull. At James Connally Air Force Base (AFB), Waco, Texas, I'd received ground school and my initial flight training to become a Radar Observer (RO). The airborne training took place in the back of a WWII Mitchel B-25 twin engine aircraft. Two students

WWII Mitchell B-25

and an instructor sat at their radar equipped stations. We took turns directing the pilot up front to take turns, climb, descend, increase speed, and throttle-back; all to practice intercepting other B-25's acting as bogeys (unknown or unfriendly aircraft).

At my graduation ceremony, 23 March 1953, they pinned on my silver wings and gold bars for my commission as 2nd Lieutenant. My new orders read: "Travel to Moody AFB, Valdosta, Georgia for Advanced All-Weather Jet Interceptor Training." Our equipment was the "hot" new Lockheed jet F-94C *Starfire*. It was a first transonic jet, and had top speed of 585 mph. Each wing carried 24 air-

1

Black Watch Diary

Lockheed F-94C Starfire

to-air "mighty mouse" rockets. The *Starfire* climbed at just under 8,000 feet per minute. For short runways, after touchdown, we'd pop the drogue parachute (cone-shaped) to help slow the aircraft from its high landing speed. Flying this aircraft was compared to having "a tiger by the tail," or a one-legged man trying to make it through the game of "hot oven," where the victim would hop on one leg as fast as possible through the gauntlet of kids lined up to spank him.

    I'd hooked up with the pilot member of our two-man crew, Al "Foots" Kramer. Al had a heavy foot on the brakes trying to prevent the F-94C from going over the end of a short runway. He'd burned out a number of tires and acquired the title of *foots* (see Epiloque for more about Al). With my size 13 flying boots, I earned the handle of *feets*; henceforth our team, became *foots and feets*.

    During a rapid descent from altitude both of my ear drums burst. On January 21st 1954, with six weeks to heal and having to visit the flight surgeon once a week, I had time to meet Naunie Wright at a VSC (Valdosta State College) social at the *Cabin-in-the-Woods*. VSC rules stated, "No dating men from Moody AFB."

Josh Batchelder

To avoid being caught, Miss Naunie signed-out as dating Josh Hedges. Her housemother never found Josh Hedges listed when she checked the Moody Base Locator. Nearly every day of the next two months, we took walks, went to dances, and saw all the local movies. By the shores of nearby Twin Lakes, we read *The Prophet* by Kahlil Gilbran. Soon we were driving back to Elberton, in Northeast Georgia, to announce to Naunie's parents that we were going to marry. Basically we said, we want your blessing but we don't have to have it. Naunie's father, Mr. Bob, said, "Damn Valdosta, I sent her to VSC to keep her away from all the boys at UGA!" He hadn't figured on the 5,000 eligible young men at Moody Air Base. Grandma Faircloth, the only enthusiastic member of the family, said, "Bout time she married, I was married at fifteen and started raising the first of fourteen children."

The Newlyweds
Married March 27, 1954

Two days later, Naunie, with her best friend Zelma Yarbrough as her bridesmaid, was at the altar with Reverend Frank Crowley. Best man Woody forgot to bring the ring. In the anteroom we joked while we waited for the ring. Later, witnesses to the wedding reported that they heard jaunty laughter from the groom and his best man. As soon as the messenger brought the ring, the mood changed. Sporting shiny new silver wings and fresh gold bars, Woody Ayres and I marched down the aisle in our Air Force

Al and Barbara Kramer
Married September 13, 1953

dress blues. I was touched as I said, "I do" and shed tears. After the ceremony and confetti, Woody and Margaret Ayres, themselves recently married, were joined by the younger Wright AFB family members to soap the windows and attach cans to our 1950 gray Plymouth sedan. Thus we had the traditional send-off.

Two hours later, having crossed the Georgia State line, we arrived at the Wade Hampton Hotel, Columbia, South Carolina. While we were dining in the hotel's restaurant we received a note from a couple celebrating twenty years of matrimony. "Good Luck! The entire world loves newlyweds." We newlyweds had a month honeymoon before my next duty in a remote region of Canada. Our itinerary was travel up the East Coast, stop in Washington, DC, see my brother and family in White Plains, New York, visit my aunt Ella and her family in Norwich, Connecticut and finally arrive at my hometown, Sudbury, Massachusetts.

After a time there I would depart Westover Field taking military air transport to Goose Air Base.

28 March 1954: Richmond, Virginia - Jefferson Davis Hotel

29-30 March 1954 : Washington, D.C. - The Annapolis Hotel

Amid the springtime Japanese cherry blossoms, during the days we toured the Smithsonian Institute, Lincoln Memorial, guard-changing ceremony at Arlington National Cemetery, and finally, the Washington Monument. Evenings, we dined and danced in the Coral Room.

31 March 1954: White Plains, New York – Midnight.

After wining and dining with my brother Johnny, and his wife Bunny, we wound our way through the snow-covered vacant city streets of White Plains. As we drove back to the Roger Smith Hotel, light snow continued making our surroundings a magical crystalline scene. The phone was ringing as we entered our room. The front desk told me that police Captain Johnny Dole was in the lobby wanting to talk with me. I changed into my Air Force dress uniform and headed down to meet Captain Dole. He asked, "Did you know that you went down a one-way street, did a U-turn, and went through a red light?" I didn't remember doing all those things. I made some reference to our being on our honeymoon, before I had to leave my bride and head overseas to Labrador, and that we'd just come back from visiting my brother. A few details from him and my memory block faded. I said, "You're right, Captain." He replied, "Go on Lieutenant. Thanks for serving our country."

Josh Batchelder

1 April 1954: White Plains, New York - Roger Smith Hotel
    We had breakfast in bed and lounged throughout the day. Before departing for the dinner party at Johnny's in-laws, we placed our champagne bottle in the bathroom basin under running water to cool it for our return later that evening. Mr. and Mrs. Lloyd H. Bunting met us at their door and led us to the living room to join my brother, Johnny, Bunny and their two daughters Janey and Marcey. We opened more wedding gifts, including a breakfast set and fine dinnerware. After a regal evening meal we headed back to the Roger Smith. Approaching our room from down the hall, we noticed water coming out from under the door. Once inside, we stepped into soaking wet plush carpet. Our cardboard boxes of wedding gifts were all wet. The plug in the bathroom basin had somehow reseated itself and allowed several hours of water to overflow. The night manager arrived to suggest that we should, "Reimburse the hotel for the cleanup cost. The room below you has water coming through the ceiling." I explained, "This whole thing is just an accident. You must have insurance to cover your cost." We evacuated our room and relocated at the nearby Westchester Motel. The following day at Mitchel Field, Long Island, New York, we took in the show, "Hell and High Water."

3 April 1954: Mitchel Field, LI, N.Y. - Transient Quarters
    We visited Times Square and went to the top of the Empire State Building. Naunie had her first visit to an Automat. We put our coins into slots below windows that allowed us to see our selected foods. We opened the small doors and retrieved our foods. All day it was very, very cold. Naunie said, "This is the coldest day I've ever known." Back at Mitchel Field we ate breakfast at the BX (Base Exchange). Later we took in a movie at the Base Theater, "The Murders in the Rue Morgue" by Edgar Allen Poe.

4 April 1954 Norwich, Connecticut
    We arrived at Aunt Ella and Uncle Tom's chicken farm. Naunie said, "I'm 'pooped' from all the New York and Connecticut traffic and parkways. I was brought up in a small Georgia town." I said, "Pooped is the right word. Summers we six children were dropped off here at the chicken farm to give my mother a respite. It was during the Depression. In bare feet we had to walk, carefully through the chicken yard to avoid all the fresh chicken poop. We fed the chickens and picked up their eggs. We learned how to chop off the heads then dump the chickens into steaming hot water before plucking their feathers."

Black Watch Diary

5 April 1954: Norwich, Connecticut - Aunt Ella's Chicken Farm
This time we are picking up wedding gifts instead of eggs. At Cousin Eleanor and Ted Montgomery's home we received more gifts. Naunie loved the beautiful green rolling hills of the Connecticut countryside.

6 April 1954: Sudbury, Mass. - My Hometown and Mother's Place.
I wrote in my diary:

> Youth in her eye, fire in her heart,
> Was ever a young soul as much in part?
> They call her childlike, my "doodlebug"
> And have the constant urge to hug
> But many is the girl of an older age
> That runs to find help in this little sage
> In all she does there's swiftness.

19 April 1954: Sudbury, Mass. - Mother's Place
We visited Paul Ecke, the German owner of the local Swedish restaurant. I used to work for him, mowing lawns, washing dishes and caring for his animals and birds. He fed me delicious meals, like roast duck and delightful desserts. After Mr. Ecke fed us and handed Naunie our wedding gift, he took her aside and told her that the way to keep Josh happy and honest and enjoy a long marriage would be "Keep him milked."

20 April 1954: Sudbury, Mass. - Mother's Place
Mother held a birthday party for me. With Naunie, Johnny and Bunny there were my sister Emmie and her daughter, Sharon, and my sister Nancy.

21-26 April 1954: Sudbury, Mass. - Camping at Mother's Place
Since there is no dependent housing at Goose Air Base, I wouldn't be able to take Naunie with me. Naunie didn't want to go back home to Georgia into her old mold, so I arranged an apartment for her in Boston. She would be with my sister Nancy, who was finishing her college semester. Later, Georgia would call her back home.

Josh Batchelder

27 April 1954: Westover Field, Mass., -Transient Quarters

My last evening with Naunie before departure for Labrador. We dined at the Officers Club (O-Club). We'd been married just one month.

Climbing out from Westover Field in a MATS (Military Air Transport Service) C-54 we passed over my hometown. Later we would fly over my mother's birth place, Nova Scotia, Pictou County, Canada, overlooking Prince Edward Island. I reflected about my flight training. At Moody, Al "Foots" Kramer had given me my first jet fighter ride. Its purpose was to convince me of his flying skills. He took us through a series of acrobatic maneuvers such as split-S's, barrel-rolls and loops. To counteract the effects of six to seven g-pressure forces, I wore a partial pressure suit. I experienced weightlessness when we topped-out of climbs. For my body, this was an all new experience. That night, after my first jet acrobatic flight, I relived all those new physical pressure changes on my body. When opening my eyes, the playback stopped. Upon closing my eyes, the playback continued. I didn't sleep the entire night. Never again would the biggest, baddest roller coaster ride impress me.

Looking ahead, I considered my new challenges: Remote duty for a year and leaving Naunie back home. The Goose Air Base Commander and Chaplain were the only two having Base quarters for dependents.

Forty-five minutes before landing, we passed over Nova Scotia's Pictou County and Prince Edward Island. After four hours flying, our C-54 transport aircraft approached and with one bounce settled onto Ernest Harmon's runway, Stephenville, Newfoundland. This was the end of my first leg north en route to Goose Air Base, Labrador.

Looking out the window, I viewed (on the ramp) our sister squadron's aircraft, the Northrop F-89C *Scorpion*, all part of our 33rd Fighter Wing. Stories of their wings coming off in flight made me glad my new duty would be flying Lockheed F-94B jets.

29 April 1954: Harmon Air Base, Newfoundland

Over the next few days awaiting a hop further north, I walked to explore the dirt roads of Stephenville, Newfoundland. It was rainy, windy, and chilling cold. I chuckled as I thought, "This is May." Everywhere around me were numerous round black rocks, nothing but rough hilly terrain with scrubby, short trees dotting the landscape. It was desolate.

Black Watch Diary

1 May 1954: Harmon Air Base - O-Club

At the O-Club I played Black Jack and lost ten cents. Then, with a new acquaintance, Brad Webster, I enjoyed several games of Chess. Toward the end of the day it was Ping Pong. Someone said the guys at Thule Air Base were the best at Ping Pong. They beat the men at Narsaserack, who beat the Airmen at Sondrestrom, who bested the Goose flyers. Goose beat those at Harmon; in turn Harmon prevailed over the troops at Presque Isle, Maine. This was obviously a myth. The degree of difficulty was also measured by the number of cans of beers consumed by the players. Credit was given for each can of beer consumed.

2 May 1954: Harmon Air Base - Local Flights

In the Base Ops Squadron Douglas C-47 aircraft, Commander, Major Butts, gave me the opportunity to log some Visual Observer (VO) time. This flight assured me of getting my flight pay for the month. Four hours per month was the minimum necessary. Our scramble sorties often were likely to run an hour or less, so if it was quiet on our alert watch, we'd need to take other aircraft flying time opportunities.

3 May 1954: Harmon Air Base -Reading *General Semantics.*

Most of the day I read material from the *International Society for General Semantics.*

4 May 1954: Harmon Air Base

In a Douglas C-54 Transport we flew a Round Robin trip to Nova Scotia and back. I logged 4+25 (four hours and twenty-five minutes flight time) as VO viewing Newfoundland and Nova Scotia. At the O-Club I was invited to participate in some square dance routines by Lt. Colonel Carter and his wife.

Josh Batchelder

Northrop F-89D *Scorpion*

Lookheed F-94B

Two

Northwest to Goose Air Base

5 May 1954: 0900 Hours Airborne over Newfoundland

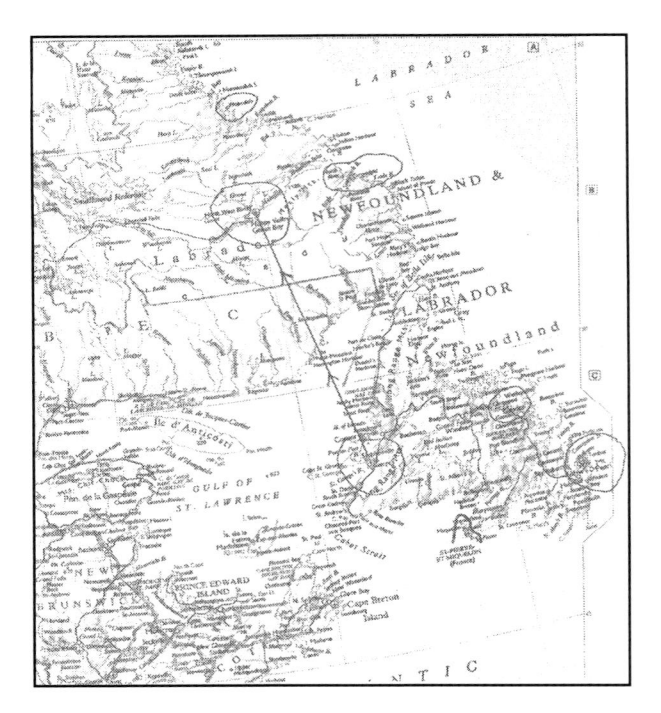

Our C-54 Transport, heavily loaded with supplies and passengers, cleared the base runway and began its climb to our assigned altitude. As we made a gentle turn north northwest from Harmon and throttled back at cruise altitude, I took out the guidebook I'd purchased at the Base Exchange and began to read about the people of Labrador and the climate.

Four distinct and separate cultures inhabit the region: The Inuit, the Innu, the Metis, and the Settlers.[3] In Labrador, the first three of the above are called aboriginal people. Labrador West and the Straits, being close to Quebec, have a French presence.

Josh Batchelder

Archaeological evidence points to the Innu ancestors being in Labrador 7,000 years ago. Innu means "human being." European settlers called them Indians. The Innu were traditionally nomadic. They hunted caribou in the winter and moved toward water in the summer to fish.

The Labrador Metis Nation is of mixed descent, having Inuit, Innu, French, Scottish, Irish and English origins. Their largest concentration is in central and southern Labrador, from Lake Melville down to Mary's Harbor and the Straits. They, like the Innu, adopted the aboriginal life to survive on the subarctic land. In 1941, many Metis and Intuit families moved to work temporarily, then permanently, constructing, and then helping to maintain Goose Air Base. They lived in Happy Valley. The settlers are identified with non-aboriginal ancestry. Later, they called themselves "Labradorians." Many were of European descent. In the 1760's the Moravians made their way to the northern and coastal part of Labrador and built missions. So the chief attractions for hardy settlers in Labrador came down to abundant fishing grounds and a bountiful supply of animals for fur trading.

Naturally, I was curious about what extremes in weather I might experience.[4] The answer came from averaging the reported statistics of the recent years. January weather was normally the meanest month. The lowest average temperature being about minus six degrees Fahrenheit (-21 degrees celsius). The average daily high was about 11 degrees Fahrenheit (-12 degrees celsius). The average snow fall in January was just under four feet, but with several feet average accumulations for November and December. These months' temperatures remaining well below freezing, I could envision plenty of packed snow by the end of January, maybe four to five feet. This mental image made me think of Buffalo, New York.

Out the window of our MATS C-54 aircraft I saw nothing but snow-covered rugged hilly terrain with rivers and lakes everywhere. Rarely did I see any smoke or other signs of human activity. Fastening my seat belt to land at my new home base on the Goose, things looked rather bleak. The Base was covered with packed deep dirty snow. The scattered scrubby trees looked like midgets. The only welcome was a sign over the entrance to Base Operations. Captain Hays, of the 59th Fighter Squadron, met me at Base Operations and gave

Plenty of Snow

me a brief tour of the base and what to expect - plenty. Tomorrow, we'll meet at the alert hangar at 0900 hours.

The Goose

In Bob Russell's book, <u>Touching The Face of God</u>, he wrote his first impression on the approach to landing at Goose: *"We are a thousand miles from the nearest city, and looking below it is difficult to see how anything could survive in this vast and motionless icescape. Then we are passing over a frozen lake, powdered with snow. As we descend, I see nothing but trees and white fields...I wonder how we can land in all this snow...ahead I notice huge hangars, huddled Quonset huts, and the tower...I shade my eyes and stare at the runways. They are also white, covered with ice and snow. Along both sides of the runway are ten foot banks of snow, blown by the snow plows as they continually clear the runway. Cut evergreen trees protrude from the snow banks, stuck there to give the pilots depth perception as they land."*[5]

Three

When The Ducks Walk, We Fly!

6 May 1954: 59th FIS (Fighter Interceptor Squadron) - Alert Hangar

The sign over the entrance to the alert hangar read, **When The Ducks Walk At Goose, We Fly!** In the squadron briefing room, my flight leader Captain Hays began with, "You're lucky…last winter on red alert, waiting on the order to scramble, we had to sit in the cockpit and freeze. Now we've got this new hangar for our alert aircraft and crews. Once we get the order to scramble, we jump into a warm cockpit and strap-in. Next, to push the snow away, the front and back hangar doors kick-out, away, and then up. We fire-up our engine and fast-taxi out to the active runway. Lighting our AB (Afterburner) we blast-off."

Foreground, the "Beater," our Wheels, and The Alert Hangar

Black Watch Diary

Captain Hays' briefing continued, "As for our status on Goose, we're tenants; our chain-of-command is direct from our 33rd Fighter Wing Headquarters at Gander, Newfoundland. They control all our air defense squadrons from Harmon to Thule, Greenland to Iceland. Across the field we've got the RCAF (Royal Canadian Air Force) operation. Tomorrow, you'll get your base orientation briefing. The job of the *ground pounders* is to support all base units and activity. As you know, SAC (Strategic Air Command) operates here, too. Goose is a refueling and emergency landing base for the great circle routes of the military and civilian arctic and transatlantic flights. Most of our air defense missions are to ID aircraft when they're off their filed flight plan course or ETA (Estimated Time of Arrival). They are allowed an ETA margin of plus or minus five minutes when entering CADIZ (Canadian Air Defense Identification Zone). Just remember, we need to get along with the *weenies* at base headquarters. Still, its Gander's orders that control us."

Captain Hays talked about the proud history of the 59th Fighter Squadron.[6] "Our unit flew the WWII P-40 Curtiss *Warhawks* supporting the North African invasion. Next, they jumped to Italy, India, Burma and China. Our men flew four thousand combat sorties in the European Theatre (ETO) and transitioned into Republic P-47 *Thunderbolts*, the Lockheed P-38 *Lightning*, and finally, in the post-war occupation of Germany, the North American P-51 *Mustang*." Captain Hays also talked about Fergus "Ferie" Fay, a WWII veteran who was an early favorite member of the 59th at Goose. Fay, Squadron C.O., flew AT-6s, P40s, P51s and P38s. (See Epilogue for excerpts from his obituary.) When J.B. Knapp, Base Commander, called upon Fergie to answer complaints about his junior officer's rebellious behavior, as a veteran WWII figher pilot he was successfully able to defend his boys.[7]

Captain Hays continued, "Now, we've got the Lockheed F-94B *Starfire*. It's the first all-weather jet interceptor with AB. When the Korean War broke out, the Air Force was in a hurry to have an all-weather and night interceptor. They began with the Lockheed T-33 two-place jet trainer airframe, and then added an AB. In the nose they placed the radar antenna and four fifty-caliber machine guns." *I thought to myself, at Moody Air Base, we trained in the latest Lockheed F-94C Starfire. It was an all new design aircraft with AB and had rocket-pods for armament in each wing.*

Captain Hays then led me to the personal equipment shop. I signed out my winter and summer flight suits, jackets, and white felt "bunny" boots. These were for the extreme temperature conditions I would face if I had to bail-out or crash-land in sub-freezing weather. Next, we went to the parachute shop where I picked up my helmet, oxygen mask and O_2 bottle, plus my survival seat-pack, which would be hooked to my parachute. With disgust, Captain Hays said, "You'll also be picking up your rubberized survival suit. It's like a heavier rubber scuba diving suit. In case you end up in the drink up here, instead of surviving five minutes, you'll freeze to

Josh Batchelder

death in about twenty. It's hell to get in and out of. If you wear it in the cockpit, you'll sweat like a pig. Most of us don't think it's worth the bother. We just take our chances. There is another reason you are lucky to be assigned here for the coming year." *Yeah, I thought to myself, a remote place with Naunie back in the States.* Captain Hays chuckled, "Last year, for housing, we had an old wooden building covered with tarpaper. We all lived there in one great big open area. It was just 18 months ago that the 59th was first assigned here. Increased threats of the Cold War and the Korean War made it necessary. Now, our new barracks quarters have room and bath for two. Last spring, our young jocks with their Rambo-like behavior got our squadron kicked-out of the O-Club (Officer's Club). However, morale really picked-up when our boys discovered space in the barracks basement. Presto! The Scramble Inn was born. Late spring, last year, after the snow melted, the Base Inspectors discovered a hoard of empty beer cans, whiskey and wine bottles scattered about. Colonel Knapp, Base Commander, summoned the whole squadron to the Base Theatre and gave us a dressing down. He turned over two six-ply trucks for the clean-up operation. For our troops, it turned into a good-time party."

Moving to the aircraft in the Scramble Hangar, Captain Hays gave me a walk around the two ready-for-flight F-94B birds. Their canopies were up. In the two cockpits, I saw survival seat packs with parachutes attached. The crews' individual helmets, with oxygen masks, were connected and ready to be donned. Next, we walked to the ready room and chatted with the two day-alert crews, Lieutenants Mac McCarthy, Bill Rutherford, Bill Taylor and Phil Gereau.

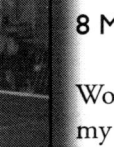

8 May 1954: 59th Fighter Squadron

I met the Adjutant, Captain Hugh Workman. Next I went to Base Finance to get my travel per diem and back pay. That evening at the O-Club I enjoyed the new fifteen piece band. In one corner our 59th party was well underway. Many of my buddies had dates.

Alert Hangar Ready Room

I took the opportunity to catch a few dances. I danced with Rita McCarthy. Rita was asked whether she would prefer a man with a mustache. She replied, "If you haven't tried it, don't knock it!" She was a TWA Flight Attendant on layover. I enjoyed another dance with Audrey Adams. She was Dave England's date from London. Frank Karpowich, RO, my friend from Connally, and I played Ping Pong. Dave Owen, a new pilot from Mississippi, arrived.

Black Watch Diary

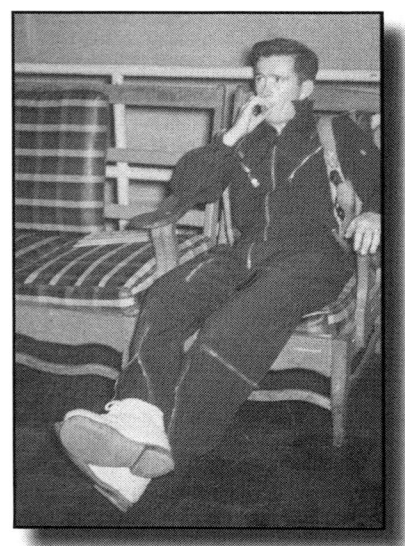

Jack Harrington in Ready Room

Belah Culpepper Playing Ping Pong in the Ready Room

Al Kramer About to Climb Ladder to Cockpit

Josh Batchelder

My experience as an enlisted man on KP (Kitchen Police) taught me how to scrounge desserts from the dining hall at Goose. I soon was delegated, when on night alert duty, to make the midnight "goody run" to the dining hall for fresh hot donuts and coffee cakes for our alert crews.

Playing Cards in the Alert Hangar Ready Room

Alert Hangar Ready Room

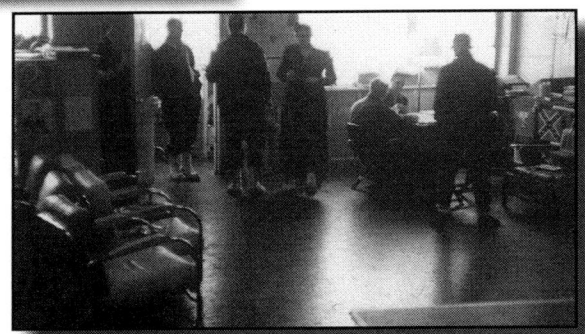

Center ROs Cockpit F-89

Four

The Scramble Inn

(Al Perry, was the first founder of the "world famous" Scramble Inn. Don Rogers sent me the story of the beginning of the Scramble Inn part of which is related below. See the end of this chapter for the whole story and the Epilogue/Legacy for more.)[8]

The Scramble Inn Was Located in the Basement of the Barracks

"*The creative resourcefulness of my squadron mates never ceased to impress me. The bar was covered with a scrap piece of commercial grade linoleum saved from the wrecking crew demolishing an old mess hall. The famous Black Bat on the bar was hand crafted from scrap plywood by Glen Paulk. The ceiling plumbing under the BOQ was dramatically screened by a superb orange and white parachute donated as condemned property by the base supply officer and put in place by Lee Grude and his happy crew of volunteers. Furniture was a possible show-stopper, there was precous little at The Goose and certainly no extras for a squadron hobby project. But the Base Housing Officer found several broken pieces of furniture in an old warehouse. He said he needed the storage space, so the pieces were ours for the taking. Avery Miller and his crew, with scrounged glue, nails, screws, wire, wook tools, and a lot of sweat, restored these relics to sturdy tables, chairs and sofas that withstood the pounding of many a squadron flight party. But the crown jewel of the decor was the ceiling light over the bar. It was the canopy of an F-94 which had been sand blasted on the inside and sprayed with a soft blue paint. It was spectacular."*

7 May 1954: Goose Air Base

After a long day of the Base orientation, I took a shower. I dressed casual and headed for the Scramble Inn in the barracks basement to join my buddies and consume some adult beverages. I heard boisterous voices down the hall, "Oh, we're the boys of 59th and we know everything. We are the joy boys of radio. We're never too busy to say hello. We're never too busy to say hello. **HELLO, HELLO, HELLO.**"

The plaque on the door of the Scramble Inn read:

There is a place named Scramble Inn
That the boys of 59th have settled in,
Where fun and frolic always win.
A grin under the wondrous warmth of a little gin.
Of course, the need of this nightly din
Finds its purpose in practices many call sin.
But, whatever the world would judge
To label this cellar retreat, with grudge,
It's the one place on Goose where a guy can let loose.

Party at the Scramble Inn

Black Watch Diary

    Remembering that our squadron once had been booted out of the O-Club, I enjoyed seeing the work on the walls of our "motivated" squadron volunteers. The decorations came with wild sayings. Paraphernalia, like model aircraft, on wires, hung from the ceiling, along with miniature parachutes. Comfortable sofas, chairs and round tables were well-placed; and, of course, there was a well-stocked bar. A welcoming committee told me about the grand opening of the past Christmas. Naturally, many of the most attractive "continental ladies" – those young women who had acquired *overnight Canadian citizenship* – helped to christen the 59th's new personal palace. Ever since, they'd received individual invitations to come and remain overnight. Barred from the youthful fun at the O-Club, the Scramble Inn was timely. Boredom was banished and morale soared. A juke box provided music for dancing. At the far end of the large room were pool and ping pong tables. Readily available were board games, Checkers, Chess and decks of cards for Poker and Bridge. *Indian Dice* a new game to me, was being played.[9] All that was required were two or more players and five dice. Mixing myself a Black Russian (vodka and Kahlua on-the-rocks), I settled in to be with new comrades and some friends I'd known from Connally and Moody training.

L to R: Lt. Col. Knapp, Base Commander, Bob Beck, Lockheed Aircraft Tech Rep., Major Voy Winders, 59th Squadron Commander

    Frank Karpowich and I played Indian Dice. We both had trained at Connally and Moody. He related an event that took place in Valdosta at an American Legion carnival, near Moody field. He and Phil Gereau were attracted to a tent that promised girls who would "bare all." The first ticket got them in to witness girlies clad in see-through black lace. It took a second fare to get behind a curtain where a big-breasted woman was standing on a stage. She waved for them to come closer and touch her and watch her do *the light a cigarette in-the-hole trick*. They both had had a few too many. Phil reached up and pulled her, by the breast, off the mini stage. We all had a good laugh about that event.

Josh Batchelder

The best story I could tell was about a Moody Air Base weekend pass caper. Tim Trebel and I decided to go to Jacksonville Beach, well beyond the fifty-mile radius war-time weekend pass-limit.[10] After parking on a sandy beach, we approached a young girl sitting on the sea wall. She was sobbing. Her twin sister had just stolen her boyfriend, and they were on their way to be married. Joking around with her, we played like we were going to throw her into the ocean. Just as we were swinging her back and forth by her arms and legs, her mother came out of their beach home and yelled, "I'm calling the cops." We dropped our playmate, and ran back to our car. It was stuck in the sand. Desperation! Inspiration came to the rescue. I put the car in low gear. With the rear wheels spinning, we went to the back bumper and rocked and pushed back and forth until we got it free. I guess being stuck in the snow and ice in my early years in New England came in handy. We jumped in and sped back across the Florida line to South Georgia and Moody. Fortunately, we avoided the double trouble possible if our Commander should ever learn about our escapade.

As that first evening in the Scramble Inn wore on, we played more Indian Dice and I heard the "skinny" on our Base Commander, Colonel J. B. Knapp. They said, "He is strict." Before he joined the Army Air Force in WWII, he'd planned to be a Fundamental Baptist Minister. We all agreed that he should have done just that. Then my comrades told me what to expect from the Base Briefing. "Watch your step, don't swear or drink too many of those special twenty-five cents cocktails at the O-Club.

Nice Party!

Stay away from the native Indians at the Happy Valley settlement. They don't have any immunity to the white man's diseases. And, oh yes, by-the-way there are two barracks full of young women workers from France, Germany, Italy, and England. Under the Native Son Agreement with Canada, the U.S. couldn't hire any non-Canadian citizens for less sensitive positions. So, under the easy immigration rules of Canada, these young women became *overnight Canadian citizens*."

My buddies went on to say, "It seems the 59th men always enjoy bending or breaking the Base rules and regulations. For example, because hot plates are a fire hazard, we aren't allowed to have them in the barracks. We hid toasters and hot plates in our closets, which is how they became pantries. When an inspection comes up, they're out of sight. On cold, wintry nights we have sumptuous hot meals and our delicious desserts. The broad outside window sills have become our freezers for quick cooling of our gelatins and a cold storage place."

Don Rogers recalled that, *"Inter-flight competition was spirited and good for morale. This included the most imaginative squadron call-signs and flight names as required by the Air Defense Command (ADC). Two original call-signs for the squadron in 1953 were 'Bucket' and 'Pintail'. Flights or individual aircraft experimented with various 'slight' changes to sound like the prescribed call sign. On most occasions, it was ignored by the tower–at other times the tower operator would come back with landing instructions broken by sporatic laugher. In 1954 'Jellybean Flight' gained fame. It did not have the heroic sound of 'Red Dog Flight' but created the proper preamble to some questionable requests;"*

"Tower, this is Jellybean Leader with a flight of two Jellybeans checking the runway to see if it is still straight before we come in to land." Then to the wingman, *"OK Jellybean Flight, kick in the afterburner and dust off the runway!"*
(*"A 'dust off' at night always included the Scramble Inn!"*)

"Several of the Jellybeans dated the young ladies of Goose, most of who were pretty Canadians. They were a spirited and joyful group who happily participated in Scramble Inn parties and song fests. They even wrote a song to Jellybean Flight."

*Here's to our boys–they are the best.
We'll take the 59th, you take the rest.
No one ever could take their place.
And what's more, they own this base.*

*As Fighter Pilots they do excel,
And as lovers, we'll never tell.
Other types are OK it seems
Till you compare them with our jellybeans.*

Josh Batchelder

When in their jets they're tigers by gad.
Watch out High Flight—they make you look sad.
RO's, Pilots—they set the pace.
And did we mention, they own this base.

Here's to the jewels—we take a drink.
There's none among them who is a fink.
They're the greatest in this place.
The 59th Fighters Own This Base.

"The Scramble Inn became well known all over the Air Force. The word was spread not only by ex-59th officers, but High Flight pilots who knew 59th pilots and were lucky enough to be invited when passing through Goose on the way to Europe. One of these High Flight Pilots in 1957 was one of the original 59th pilots who had gone to Goose with the squadron from Otis AFB in 1952. He was happy to see the squadron 'hi jinks' had not changed since his days in the 59th. The squadron operated the Scramble Inn until 30 April 1966. On 1 May, it became an annex of the Officers Club."

The Bar at the Scramble Inn

Black Watch Diary

The following account of the history of the Scramble Inn was written by Al Perry, 59th Fighter Interceptor Squadron, Goose Bay, Labrador 1953-54:

The Saga of the Scramble Inn

To fully appreciate this story and period in time, one has to understand the outpost mentality of "The Goose." Yes, there was the usual small commissary, officers' mess cafeteria, bare stud walls BOQ, and basic three service, but that was about it. If you like wilderness, you loved The Goose.; mud roads, ancient forests, caribou, Eskimos and wild critters to write home about. Mosquitoes the size of disbelief. Some boating in old scows, a little fishing, and a contrived ski hill the likes of which defied being called a "sports facility." Resort life it was not, but for those of us on flight duty and fortunate to fly off into the blue–or even a murky weather night– our F-94s were one of the few exhilarating reprieves from the mundane life of this outpost U.S. Air Force base.

The closeness of the 59th Fighter Squadron life tended to cause exaggerated behavior in our off-duty activities which were boisterous and often accompanied by song fests in the O-Club with rowdy lyrics that often ended with the phrase, "And once more we own this base!" Our fellow officers, not in our squadron, did not appreciate our claim to ownership or our uninhibited fighter squadron style.

So our story begins with the temporary banning of our squadron from the O-Club for our macho bravado conduct. We had been "grounded" from our favorite watering hole. Gloom abounded.

A New 59th "Gaggle" Club

"What are you doing down here in the basement of the BOQ, Al?"

I looked up at my old good friend and fellow pilot, Jim Rawlings, and said, "I'm building a small private club for our squadron and these 2 x 4's and scrap lumber are going to be the bar."

Rawlings stared at me with an incredulous look and asked, "How did you get approval for it?"

"You don't need approval for a hobby-project, Jim."

"Hobby project?" He queried. (This is the origin of the U.S. military's policy "don't ask, don't tell)

Jim then volunteered to help and in that bleak, small corner of the BOQ basement our private club started to take form.

Josh Batchelder

We Learn To Scrounge

The pounding of nails and sawing of wood aroused the attention of our squadron mates and soon our crew grew rather quickly. Early volunteers besides Rawlings were Lee Grude, Avery Miller, Glen Paulk, and my faithful roommate and fellow collaborator, Ken Lengfield. Before long we had horsepower to spare for our new hobby-project, The Scramble Inn! The name was an obvious choice and play on words. I knew we had a success in the making the first time I heard Dave England play a few jazz riffs on his trombone during construction – not Carnegie Hall sound, but as good as it got at The Goose.

Several serious facility questions had to be addressed, i.e., heating and ventilation, toilets, painting, furniture, floor and ceiling finishes, and the main attraction – decorating the bar, plus the not so small requirement, 'Who's going to clean up the party messes?'

We quickly learned the art of requisition from base dump piles. The Goose had a lot of heavy construction going on at the time and their dump piles were filled with quality throw away materials, so on the way from Base Ops to the BOQ we would make side stops with "The Beater", our one and only mobile unit from the motor pool. We also learned the art of Newfie bartering with our cartons of cigarettes and cases of booze as basic trading goods – our mystery building materials stockpile thrived!

Operation Improvise

The creative resourcefulness of my squadron mates never ceased to impress me. The bar was covered with a scrap piece of commercial grade linoleum saved from the wrecking crew demolishing an old mess hall. The famous Black Bat on the bar was hand crafted from scrap plywood by Glen Paulk. The ceiling plumbing under the BOQ was dramatically screened by a superb orange and white parachute donated as condemned property by the Base Supply Officer and put in place by Lee Grude and his happy crew of volunteers. Furniture was a possible show-stopper, there was precious little at The Goose and certainly no extras for a squadron hobby-project. But the Base Housing Officer found several broken pieces of furniture in an old warehouse. He said he needed the storage space, so the pieces were ours for the taking. Avery Miller and his crew with scrounged glue, nails, screws, wire, wood tools, and a lot of sweat, restored these relics to sturdy tables, chairs and sofas that withstood the pounding of many a squadron flight party. But the crown jewel of the decor was the ceiling light over the bar. It was the canopy of an F-94 which had been sand blasted on the inside and sprayed with a soft blue paint. It was spectacular! As to its source though, my fellow collaborators and I are suffering from "senior moments" as to how we came by it.

But how to turn ugly cement basement walls and floors into pleasant colors. Ken Lengfield and his crew prayed for the divine intervention of the Sherwin Williams trash pile fairy and from old buckets of yellow, green, purple, red and blue, they concocted a disco hue and "voila," perfection!

Opening Night

On Christmas Eve, 1953, The Scramble Inn held its Grand Opening. It was massively well attended. By any standard it was one of the best stocked bars in the Northeast Air Command (hey, booze was sold at "can't afford not to prices")! If the Ruskies had heard about our opening they probably would have considered it a strategic night to attack the U.S. But one flight was on alert duty to intercept any bad dudes should they decide the 59th was not in a fighting mode and to also identify the usual airliners gone astray.

Jim Rawlings, one of the original Scramble Inn founders, was one of those who found himself particularly hacked to be "Scrambled Red" on Christmas Eve, so he took it out on a wayward British Airways Stratocruiser. When flying in for an ID he saw passengers living it up in the aircraft's belly-bar. Naturally, Rawlings demonstrated his resentment with a Warp-one fly-by responded to by the Brit pilot's radio rebuke, "I say old chap…it's not my fault you missed your party!"

Great Good Luck

"Who's going to clean up the mess from the night before?" One of the more creative solutions to this operating problem proved to be one of the more competitive inter-flight rivalries. The flight off-duty who partied could leave the place trashed and the flight on night alert had to clean up the mess when they came off duty in the morning. It was always a grimacing flight group who opened The Scramble Inn door each morning to behold what the off-duty flight had accomplished…this was the beginning of "Creative Trash Art." One has to wonder what became of some of these trash artists? Oddly and humorously it became a competition to see who could leave the biggest mess without material destruction. No flight was ever declared the winner and the debate over the best trasher flight continues to this day.

Josh Batchelder

Jellybeans and the Ladies of The Goose

Interflight competition was spirited and good for morale. This included the most imaginative flight names for the day as required by the Air Defense System. The names had to be simple and communicate with clarity between airborne flight members and ground control services such as the tower, ground control radar and GCA. So, Jellybean Flight gained fame in the unique humor of its name which was part of The Goose lifestyle syndrome of this place and time. It intentionally did not have the heroic sound of "Red Dog Flight."

I can still hear them today, "Tower, this is Jellybean Leader with a flight of two Jellybeans checking the runway to see if it is still straight before we come in to land."

"OK Jellybean Flight, kick in the afterburners so we can dust off the runway." A "dust off" at night always included The Scramble Inn.

Several of the Jellybeans dated the young ladies of The Goose, most of whom were pretty Canadians. They were a spirited and joyful group who happily participated in Scramble Inn parties and song fests. They even wrote a song to Jellybean Flight. They made life at The Goose endurable!

Black Watch Diary

Scenes from the Scramble Inn

J.J. Johnston

"Sure, baby. I fly jets!"

"Think that's enough beer!?"

Jack "Maggie" McGee and
Johnny Johnston

Five

Pinetree Ground Control

12 May 1954: Goose Bay

Eight of the 59th newest aircrew members, including myself, mounted our ten-wheeler truck to travel eight miles up a winding dirt road and visit our local Pinetree GCI (Ground Control Intercept) station. It was on a hilltop just three air miles from Goose. We needed to know the men on-the-ground. They would be ordering us to "Scramble" to intercept bogey (unknown or unfriendly) aircraft entering our airspace. Major Paul Revere, the *early warning* site commander, led us through covered passageways, around the station.[11] There were two-story barracks for the personnel and over thirty double-wides for married folks. We learned about long-range surveillance radars. They detected the location of airborne craft. Height-finder radars supplied the altitude information. To prevent high wind damage, inflated rubber domes covered the antennas.

Pinetree Radar Rubber Dome

Black Watch Diary

Major Paul Revere introduced us to the day shift controllers. They were manning the radar scopes in the main building. Revere briefed us on the *big picture* of the northern North American Air Defense (NORAD) system.[12] This network spanned the Continent from the Alaskan Straits to the Atlantic and Labrador Sea leading to the Arctic Circle. Air bases were built in strategic locations beginning at Anchorage and Fairbanks, Alaska, across Canada covering what was becoming the Dewline (Distance Early Warming). Labrador, Greenland and Iceland Air Bases and their surveillance radar stations comprised our northeastern zone defense. All of this he explained resulted from the increased threats of the Korean War and the long-range bomber flights over the shorter arctic air routes. The new priorities dictated building and expanding bases, radar tracking stations, and fighter-interceptor squadrons from Ernest Harmon Air Base, Newfoundland, to Goose, to Iceland and Thule Air Base, Greenland.

About 300 military and civilian personnel operated Pinetree Station. The smaller radar sites had about 150 personnel. Because Lake Melville iced over in the winter, re-supplying Goose Bay took place between May and October. For Thule, Greenland, the supply window was much shorter. Major Revere explained that the coordination of Pinetree and Goose Air Base activity began 500 miles south of us at St. Johns, Newfoundland Headquarters. The network included Cartwright and Hopedale radar stations on the Labrador Coast. Further north, on Greenland, the system had more radar stations and defense Air Bases. Eastward some fifteen hundred miles was Reykjavik, Iceland. It had a surveillance radar station and an all-weather interceptor squadron.

I found it very interesting to learn that in 1951 it took 140 ships to transport the construction supplies and equipment to make Thule Air Base operational.[13] Thule was our northernmost defense base. It was located in the Arctic Circle. Naturally, SAC (Strategic Air Command) and ADC (Air Defense Command) operations were established there.

Major Revere warned us that air to ground communications could periodically be frustrated or prevented by magnetic atmospheric disturbances.[14] The explanation was that at different time periods and different locations around the globe, including our arctic regions, increased sun spot activity would lead to a high degree of ionization. This created an invisible wall that blocked very high frequency (VHF) transmissions. Our scientists were carrying out extensive research to resolve this problem.

I asked him about all of the above-ground water and steam heat pipes that I had seen at Pinetree and Goose Air Base. He explained that this was to avoid the damage caused by the deep frost. Shifting pressures below the surface would crush the pipes. He went on, "The modular-type buildings you see here with their passageway connections are pretty much the style for all our radar stations. In the short summer period, when Lake Melville ice has melted, most of our re-supply takes place. Fresh fruit and vegetables are regularly flown in." Following lunch at Pinetree, we began our trip back to Goose. I noticed in a small level area there was a spot for landing helicopters.

Having received the base and Pinetree orientations, it was now time for me to get familiar with the defense areas we would be flying. When defense threat levels were higher, we would be flying CAP (Combat Air Patrol) sorties that allowed for swifter intercept of unfriendlies.

In a B-25 WWII aircraft, we departed Goose for our orientation flight around the Lake Melville sectors, north and east of Goose. We winged our way eastward, over Lake Melville, bound for the Cartwright Radar Station and local Settlement. It was on the Labrador coast, about 150 miles from our home plate (air base). The local population was about five-hundred. The Settlement was established in 1775 by Captain George Cartwright[15]. He was an English sailor and trader of fish and furs. Flying low over the village we could see two cannons that had, in the early years, protected the sheltered harbor entrance. In 1837, the Hudson Bay Trading Company established its principal trading post here. It continued as a main port-of-call for shipping and fishing boats. After viewing the Settlement, we requested a low pass over the Cartwright Radar Station. Immediately, we got a "Roger" from the controllers. Several operators appeared outside to wave. At 200 feet, we flew by, gunned our engines and rocked our wings. Next, we turned north up the Labrador Sea coastline to familiarize ourselves with the Hopedale Station and Settlement. The Hopedale Community was about the same size as Cartwright. It was first established in 1782 by Moravian Missionaries.[16] Originally, it was called Agvituk, meaning, "a place where there are whales." The Hopedale Mission building was thought to be one of the oldest East of Quebec. Our low pass over the Mission building confirmed that it was still standing. We requested another low pass over the village and radar station. As soon as we got a "Roger", we gunned our engines, buzzed the site and saluted with our wings. Bound back for Goose, we turned southwest to skirt the shoreline of Lake Melville.

With my radar set controls, I tilted our nose antenna down, below the horizon, to "paint" the Lake and shoreline on my radar scope. Recognition of our map position with my Airborne Radar screen display was easy. This was because large lakes, rivers and mountains were easy to discern on the scope. More difficult to recognize on my radar screen were any less defined terrain features, such as smaller lakes, rivers, and hills. For example, frequent changes from the late spring melting of large accumulations of snow and ice radically changed the outside-the-window scene. This was due to the rapid visual changes that wouldn't match the fixed map depictions. Another complication of intercept radars was that their design was not meant for ground mapping. Normally, we would be under the control of GCI

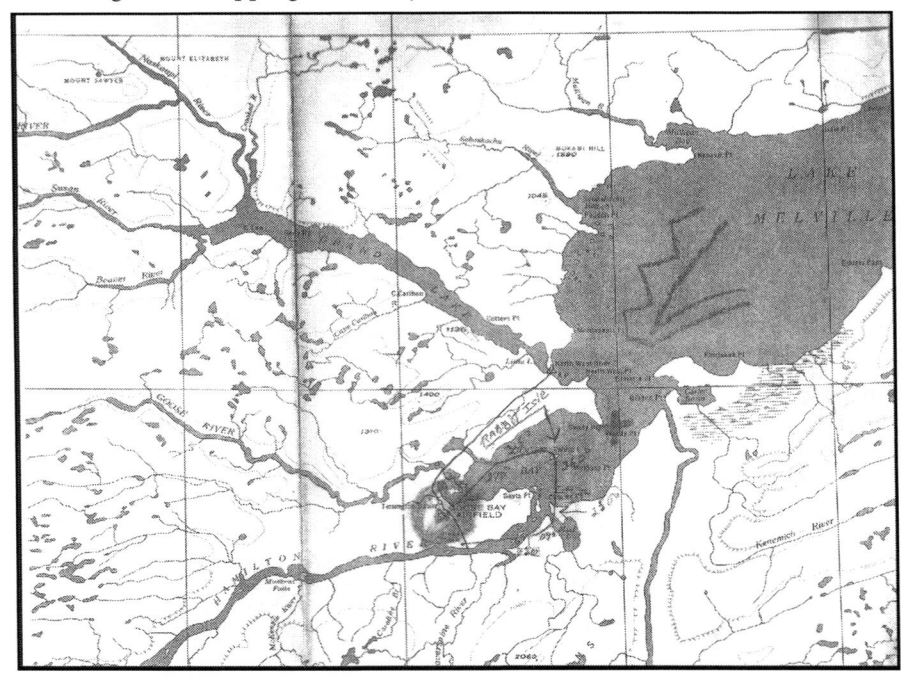

Lake Melville, Rabbit Island, and Goose Bay

who would be keeping track of our positions. It was only in an emergency when we lacked air-to-ground communications that navigating by my radar could become critical. To prepare for just such a situation, I practiced radar navigation on the long, slow final approach to landing at Goose. For the approach to Goose Air Base I had the advantage of the clear shoreline of Lake Melville. Rabbit Island, close to the Base, was the checkpoint for our radar approach to the Base. In steps, using the radar, I advised the pilot of our distances and required altitudes to the touch down zone.

After landing, I opened my log book and entered 4+30 flight time (four hours and thirty minutes). It was time for a shower, the O-Club or the Scramble Inn.

Six

Vell, Iss You From Missouri?

25 May 1954: Movie "Roman Holiday"
Liked it well enough to see twice.

30 May 1954: O-Club
Drinking burgundy wine with Gene Moen, Hird, O'Brien, Al, McNeely and "Cat" Curry, soon we were writing a song for the 59th. Two Brits visited our table and we got into a verbal contest. The table topic was Stephen Potter's book about "Lifemanship," "Gamesmanship," and "Workmanship," etc. Cat Curry said, "By the time I finished the book, I thought I was in the water with all the ships."

The O-Club

Black Watch Diary

12 June 1954: Saturday Noon - O-Club
    After our annual Base parade, we 59th flyers retired to the O-Club to sip some beers and sing some songs like, "Who owns this club, RA RA?" From their barracks, across the street from the O-Club, the girls from the continent -- *overnight Canadian citizens* -- began to arrive. They performed many of the secretarial or other non-sensitive jobs on Base. Elinear, a well-endowed miss from Heidelberg Germany strode in wearing a very revealing white angora sweater. She leaned over our table, and sweetly said to our leader, Captain Hays, "Hello." He'd been leading us in wild songs. He said, "Are they for real?" In her heavy German accent she replied, "Vell, iss you from Missouri?"

    From the O-Club many of us headed back to our Scramble Inn for more songs, dancing, and drinking. A number of the girls accepted invitations to follow us back to the barracks and the Scramble Inn. I got a chance to dance with Shep's date, Joan MacDonald. It felt good to hold a woman in my arms.

    With more drinks we began to compose some poetry:

Now after a little whiskey
A fellow's bound to be frisky
So, what's awaiting the call but a girl all dressed for a ball
And, really not sure at all what's likely to happen in a fall
And, whether the past's beyond recall.
Now, our 59th has a special beater
That's meant to carry girls, like Anita
Down the dusty trail to a far corner of the base
Where we all can begin our merry little chase
Now there's one dark room in our place
Where the sin is to light up a disgrace
And disturb the ones holding a current case;
Who are naturally making their darndest haste.
But let's not linger in this room,
Unless we've our own little bunny to caress.

Seven

Scramble, Crash, and Burn

19 June 1954 Goose Air Base Flight Line, 1800 hours
It was evening, and time for the alert duty shift change. Al and I removed our parachutes, helmets, and oxygen masks from our cockpits. Pilot, Bill Rutherford, and RO, Mac McCarthy, set up their cockpits for their Black Watch duty. Moments later, we heard the Scramble alarm go off. We saw Bill and Mac fast taxi to the active runway, go to full power and light their Afterburner. As they broke ground and began their climb, we saw a long blast of rocket-like flame coming from their tail pipe. It looked at least as long as the length of their fuselage. At about 300 feet on a heading of 308 degrees they attempted a 180 degree turn back to the field. We saw them sinking into the boonies. A cloud of smoke appeared. We heard the rescue team being activated. The next day we visited Bill and Mac's hospital room and learned the rest of the story. After crashing, their canopy wouldn't eject. Their bird caught on fire. In a circle into his overhead canopy, Mac fired five 357 Magnum slugs from his pistol. He reloaded and fired three more into the canopy. With his helmet on, Mac busted through the canopy. He pulled the outside fuselage canopy release and lifted the canopy to pull Bill from their burning aircraft. The weird thing about the accident and escape was that Mac carried his 357 Magnum pistol in a shoulder holster in case he would ever need it to get out of the cockpit. "But for the Grace of God I'd have been trapped in the cockpit without a means of escape."[17]

20 June 1954
I played an early morning game of Poker with Bergstrom. He explained some fine points about the game. I lost seven dollars. I'll just eat less till pay day. I estimated my net gambling losses for the month at five dollars.

Black Watch Diary

21 June 1954

At the morning meeting of our squadron in the Hangar Ops Briefing Room, Major Davidson, our new Squadron Commander, said, "I believe Lt. Rutherford and McCarthy's accident was the result of pilot error." Lockheed aircraft and Allison tech reps spoke about our aircraft systems. Captain Saylor said, "Let's not get into maintenance policy when we talk about the AB (After Burner)." I understood that when Bill came out of AB, after becoming airborne, that the AB eyelids (the end of tailpipe) failed to close, resulting in the loss of power that led to the crash. Following our flight crews' meeting, I had a great game of chess with Al; and later at the Base hobby shop finished building two filing cabinets and a telephone table.

22-28 June 1954

During this quiet period I read *Point Counter Point* by A. Huxley, *Proverbs of a Humanist* by A. Guerrard, and saw "The Bigamist" at the Base Theatre.

Aerial View of Goose Air Base

Eight

Chasing Flying Saucers

30 June 1954 - Evening Shift, Airborne on Combat Air Patrol

GCI directed Al and me to investigate the flying objects sighted by the crew of a British Airways *Connie* near the Labrador coast. They reported seeing one large black craft with six smaller ones, in tow. About thirty miles from the bogeys they appeared on my radar scope. I initiated commands to intercept them. Approximately five miles off our wing we visually observed the "saucers."[18] Before we could get a closer look, they streaked away, extremely fast. We told GCI what I had observed on the radar and our visual observation. It didn't look like any weather phenomenon. After landing we filed our report. Even though we were on the night shift, it was still daylight because of summer in the higher latitudes.

7 July 1954

We heard that the St. John's Newfoundland newspaper had covered the flying saucer story as reported by the British Airways captain.[19]

9 July 1954, Goose

Just after Al and I got off Day-Alert, a Continental Air Defense exercise got underway.

10 July 1954, The Northeast Command Defense Exercise continued:

I flew three sorties with Pappy Brims. We intercepted a B-36 Bomber, an SA-16 search and rescue craft, an Israeli *Connie,* and a C-119 *Flying Boxcar.* The SAC B-36 was at 6,500 feet in the clouds and rain. It was trying to evade detection by sneaking into Goose at a low level. Ground surveillance radars have difficulty picking up low level flying aircraft.

Black Watch Diary

11 July 1954, Defense Readiness Test continued:
    Poor weather conditions, gusty winds, and rain showers combined with multiple incursions by different aircraft types flying at varying altitudes, really tested our readiness. Cagey planning by SAC was evident throughout this whole exercise.

12-13 July 1954, Quiet Period on Goose:
    During the quiet periods I read William James *Death and the Value of Life*, and *The Realities of Religion*. I wrote in my diary:

> *The crowd and mob are alike; they are each a personal assemblage, for a single occasion having an absence of reflection and discussion…motivated by emotion and impulse…individual members are so merged with the whole, as to be dominated by collective emotion…when the crowd changes from passive state, or mere interaction to a state of aggressive collective action to some unreasoned objective, they become a mob.*

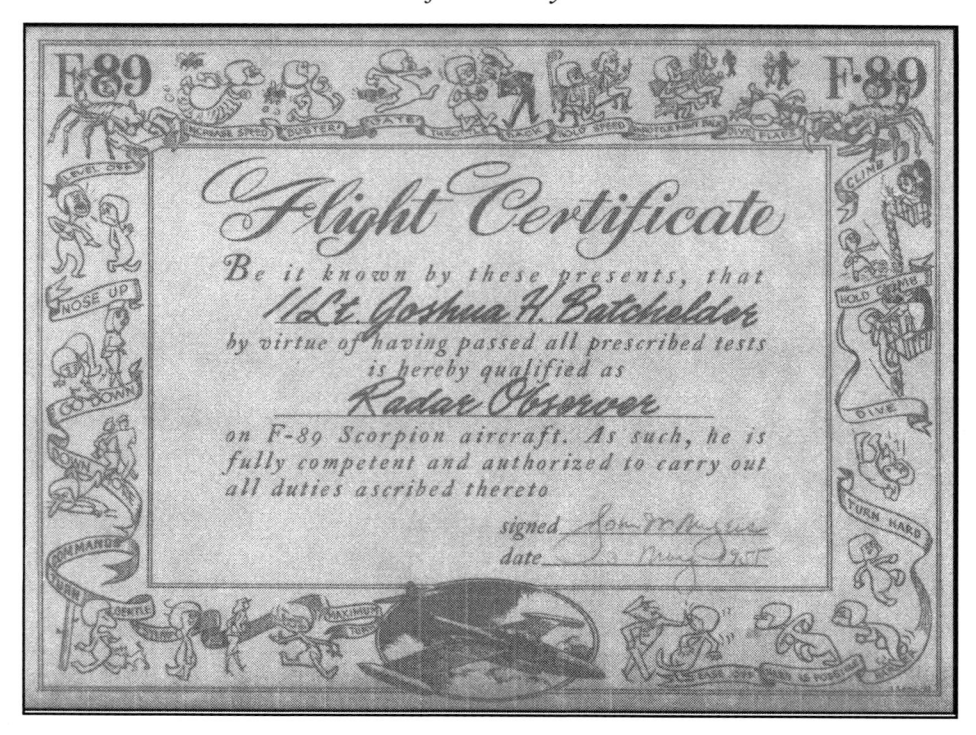

Nine

Flame-out! Angels Twelve

14 July 1954:
    At 1505 hours, Lieutenants Clark and RO, Gaddess, on their return to Goose, experienced a flame-out at 12,000 feet. Their seat ejection system failed to blow. Clark raised their canopy with their emergency hand crank. Gaddess bailed out at 4,500 feet. Their bird crashed in the trees. A small boy spotted Gaddess' parachute and told his dad. They came across the river in their motorboat to pick up Gaddess. Rex Winchell recalled that "RO Gaddess lost his gloves when he popped the canopy. His hands were so numbed (sub-freezing temperatures and wind blast hitting the cockpit) that he couldn't pull the ejection seat trigger. He bailed out over the side and got one of his legs badly broken when it hit the vertical stabilizer."

15 July 1954:
    The next day, talking with Gaddess, we learned that Clark rode their ship down. Did his seat fail to eject? Gaddess said they had planned to bail out at 6,000 feet. In spite of the variable 600 to 1500 foot cloud ceiling, did Clark try to ride his bird in? To restore our confidence, *will our squadron maintenance now check out all the seat and canopy ejection systems?*
    I'm reading *Education*, it's about circular reasoning and causal assumptions, by William James. Events and circumstances, occurring at the same time, often get confused with cause and effect, rather than being coincidental. Thus, there is confused thinking and false conclusions and myths that can arise within a group. So, every accident needs to be explored thoroughly before we jump to conclusions.

17 July 1954:
    We had an O-Club dance and then we moved our 59th party to the Scramble Inn. On the way down to Scramble Inn, I saw M... exiting his room with J....

Black Watch Diary

following. He said, "We've just been thrilling in the joys of copulation, Josh." Later, he said, "It's nice to date someone with a small vocabulary." I catch the subtlety of his remark. Late afternoon, I won $8.50 at Indian Dice.

18 July 1954:

I went to the morning church service. In the late afternoon, we all attended a service for Lt. Clark. *How come there was no flag at half-mast?* In the evening while playing Indian Dice I began letting go of our loss. I won $4.50.

19 July 1954:

Down in the Scramble Inn we played Penny Poker. I won $2.40. Later I read a Reader's Digest article, "Man's Unconquerable Mind," by Gilbert Highet, a Scottish Professor at Columbia University.

20 July 1954:

At the Base Gym I worked out with Al and Bill Taylor. Afterwards, we ate at the O-Club and returned to the Scramble Inn to play Indian Dice. I won $6.00. We saw the movie, "About Mrs. Leslie" starring Shirley Booth. A new pilot, Lt. Don Leonard, arrived from Langley Field, Virginia. He said, "Your classmate, Joe Jevnick, is the Supply Officer at Langley; and, another of your Connolly classmates, John Noyes, got assigned to Presque Isle, Maine, and then Thule, Greenland."

> The favorite squadron patch of the black bat across a yellow moon was universally accepted by aircrews; however, it wasn't registered with the Air Force, so the old lion patch with the phrase "Golden Pride" is official.

Freicudan Du: Gaelic for "Black Watch"

Ten

The Scorpions Are Coming

22 July 1954: 59th Ops Briefing, F89D Briefing.

Northrop Aviation Salesman, Mr. Mathins, gave us the F-89D *Scorpion* specifications: "Its range of 2,600 miles is more than double your 94s. Its speed is well over 600 mph. It packs a wallop with its 104 air-to-air 'mighty mouse' rockets in its wing-tip pods. Its like a football field of rockets fired at the enemy." Answering questions about our new birds to arrive November 11th, he said, "You'll find their cockpits roomy." I remembered how cramped I felt in our F94Bs when I first arrived on Goose and I had to turn my size thirteen bunny boots sideways because they wouldn't fit straight. Also the radar set, when down in my lap to operate, or even when placed in the up-position, extended over my knees. If I was forced to eject, I feared my knees would strike the metal housing holding the radar set and scope. When I told Major Roy Winders, Squadron Commander, about the problem, he said, "We can assign you to the F89C Squadron at Harmon Newfoundland. Those RO cockpits would fit you well." A few stories about their wings coming off in flight made my decision. I'd stay with the 59th and the Lockheed F94Bs cramped cockpit. Most of us said if you had to crash land, Lockheed's cockpits would hold up well and protect you.

We threw a party at the Scramble Inn for the Northrop salesman and his Hughes Aircraft Associate rep., whose company provided our advanced radar equipment. During the evening I talked with Mimi. She wondered about ethics, ideas, and our opinion of the girls at Goose compared with those stateside. She's from Halifax, Nova Scotia, and has seen Picton County where my mother was from. She said, "You helped me a lot to put into words my thinking." Her mother and father are poets, writers and teachers.

Black Watch Diary

Northrop F-89D Scorpion

24 July 1954: Saturday Evening - O-Club Entertainment.
The Melody Maids entertained us at the O-Club. They were twenty-three girls from Beaumont, Texas. Their ages ranged from 17 to 22. They traveled throughout the US and around the world with tours and productions for servicemen's clubs.

25 July 1954: Sunday Morning.
The Melody Maids visited our flight line and hangar to learn about our air defense mission of intercepting unknown aircraft coming over the CADIZ territory. Demonstrating a scramble alarm, Lt. Harrington, while *The Melody Maids* watched, fell on his face climbing up the ladder to the cockpit.

Josh Batchelder

Al and I scrambled on a chaff mission (bits of aluminum strips thrown or shot out of an aircraft to spoof airborne and ground radars). This chaff can spread out over many miles across the sky and descend slowly confusing radar operators about what they are seeing, aircraft or chaff. That evening we watched the movie "The Magnificent Obsession."

26 July 1954: O-Club Evening.
I saw "The Glenn Miller Story" again, and liked the theme and music. Earlier in the day, I visited the crew on-board a KC-97 tanker parked on the flight line by Base Ops. They are stationed at Harmon and serve SAC.

27 July 1954: O-Club.
After seeing the "Air Force Story," I played some Bridge. I must read some of Culbertson or Gorin to improve my Bridge game.

29 July 1954:
Movie this evening, "Her Twelve Men," starring Greer Garson. It was very good. It was all about *The Oaks School For Boys*.

30 July 1954: Cross country flight-of-four to Harmon Air Base.
Four air crews, including O'Brien and Curry, Stegner and Thomas, Taylor and Gereau, and Al and I, participated in the mission. Upon our return flight-of-four to Harmon, we approached Goose airfield in tight formation. We performed an excellent formation, passing by the tower before our sharp up wind break for final approach and landing. Goose tower operators gave us high praise.

1 August 1954: Sunday, O-Club.
I served with a group of officers completing an inventory of the O-Club. It lasted four hours and was led by Lt. Gardner.

That evening in the Ballroom at the Club they had a combo that played our favorite songs. Shephard and I talked about the discovery of one's own ethics and lifestyle choices. I told him that I especially liked the philosopher, Henry David Thoreau saying, "Thus men will lie on their backs and talk about the fall of mankind; and, never even make an effort to get up."

Eleven

A Bun in the Oven?

5 August 1954: Goose Air Base
After reading *The Loved One* by Evelyn Waugh, I expressed feelings in my diary:

> *There're northern lights, tonight honey*
> *In a sky that few hours ago was sunny*
> *And my love is not in sight to enjoy with me, twilight*
> *I'd as soon there was no fight*
> *But what can I do a little mite*
> *Except continue to play the part of flight*
> *In a service to protect this nation's plight*
> *Yet, would my honey know tonight*
> *That all I wish and thinks right*
> *Is to hold her again at night*
> *In my arms, soft and tight.*

6 August 1954:
Movie, "Gunga Din," 'twas good.

7 August 1954:
Read, *The Proper Study of Mankind* by Stephen Chase. It includes anthropology, psychology, sociology, economics, and political science plus, math, statistics, logic and semantics writers: Ogden, Richards, Korzybski, Hayakawa, and Johnson.

Josh Batchelder

11 August 1954: Diary Entry.

Statement of Human Rights submitted to UN by American Anthropological Association:

1. That the individual realizes his personality through his culture. Hence respect for individual differences entails a respect for cultural differences.
2. Respect for differences between cultures is validated by the scientific fact that no technique of qualitatively evaluating cultures has been discovered.
3. Standards and values are relative to the culture from which they derive. Any attempt to extend the beliefs or moral codes of one culture must weaken the applicability of any declaration of human rights to mankind as a whole.

14 August 1954: Saturday Evening at the Scramble Inn.

Captain Aiman walked into our 59th party and related tales of his overseas experiences during WWII. Now, here we are again at war, and I'm in it. Earlier today I flew a test hop with Captain Bassett. We had beaucoup maintenance write-ups to log including the right wing tip tank cowling, inside and under; it had come loose, so we dropped the tank over water.

15 August 1954:

The Base Chaplain, Reverend John Betterman, launched into a lecture on the evils of liquor and lascivious behavior at Goose. In the afternoon I read more on general semantics. For example, the types of "semantic blockages: "Confusing words with things and levels of abstraction; also the inability to distinguish between a fact and inference. Then there's faith in absolutes as a failing. Leaving important characteristics out. False identification. The pursuit of meaningless questions. Semantics has three primary aims: 1. Help individuals think straighter. 2. Improve communication between individuals and groups. 3. Cure abnormal mental conditions. My diary continued to describe how signs and symbols, including words, may be said to have meaning; and, how semantics helps us to understand the interrelationships of language and behavior.

On the less serious side, we exchanged jokes over a few drinks. Question: What did the Queen of England say to the Duke of Edinburgh? "Mountbatten, the whole of England is yours." Then another buddy volunteered, "There was a French politician who went around kissing unborn babies."

Black Watch Diary

18 August 1954:

I began with more reading in Stephen Potter's book about *Lifemanship and Gamesmanship*. Later in the evening I saw a movie starring Robert Young, Jimmy Stewart, and Rosalind Russell, "The Guy with a Grin."

20 August 1954:

Movie, Debbie Reynolds in "Susan Slept There." It was funny.

21 August 1954: Sunday.

I'm studying Margaret Mead's book, *Male and Female*. I played Bridge in the afternoon followed by Chess, then watched Marlon Brandon and Eva Marie Saint in "On the Waterfront."

23 August 1954:

Received a letter from Naunie saying that she'd gotten an "engraved invitation" from Colonel James B. Knapp, Goose Base Commander. She would be staying for several weeks at the Degink Hotel. She would be arriving August 31st at MCA, the civilian terminal Canadian side of Goose.

31 August 1954:

Amidst snow flurries, Naunie arrived at Goose. I was on alert. My buddies picked her up and took her to the O-Club. They entertained Naunie and delayed for a while telling me that she had arrived. Subsequently, we moved into the Degink. From the fancy invitation, Naunie had envisioned a plush hotel suite. What we found was different. We entered the front door of an old WWII Army barracks. Wooden orange crates served as table and chairs; and, two army cots tied together became our marriage bed.

3 September 1954:

Sue, Dave White's wife, arrived at Goose and they settled into the Degink Hotel in a suite down the hall. We all went to the Scramble Inn and arrived before the party began.

Josh Batchelder

5 September 1954: Evening at the O-Club.
Naunie and I watched the movie, "Sabrina," starring William Holden, Audrey Hepburn, and Humphrey Bogart. We had supper with Don Wilson. He mentioned his recent marriage was like ours. It was a war-time short courtship. His wife is now living in Thomasville, Georgia. He showed us his picture of his nineteen-year-old bride.

6 September 1954:
I began reading Bertrand Russell's, *A History of Western Philosophy*.

12 September 1954, My diary entry:
Many superstitions result from hasty post hoc reasoning. For example, someone sees a Black person. Later in the day, he loses his pocketbook. A connection is assumed; a prejudice has begun. Most of us average a misfortune or two every day of our lives.

Some tips on straight thinking:

- Something happens and presently something else happens. It looks as if the first causes the second, but actually it doesn't.

- Even more commonly, event A may affect B, but in a minor way, only as part of a process which includes other causes.

- Or, trends A and B may move together, but it is difficult to tell which is cause and which is effect.

14 September 1954 – More Diary Entries
- Sympathy is never wasted, except when you give it to yourself.

- If you never stick your neck out, you'll never get your head above the crowd.

- The enemy of the best is not the worst but the good enough.

- There are in nature neither rewards nor punishment, there are consequences.

- Don't find fault, find a remedy. Anybody can complain.

Black Watch Diary

16 September 1954:
Reading *Adventures in Genius* by Will Durant.

18 September 1954:
I read Herbert Hoover's *The Protection of Freedom* in the latest issue of Reader's Digest. The following was an extract, *The Common Man* – "the greatest strides of human progress have come from uncommon Men and Women. The humor of it is that when we get rich we want an uncommon doctor. When we go to war, we want an uncommon general or admiral. When we choose a president of a university, we want an uncommon educator."

23 September 1954:
Movie, "Executive Suite" by T.S. Eliot.

26 September 1954:
Saw a movie, "The Caine Mutiny" featuring Mel Ferrer.

27 September 1954: Evening time at The Scramble Inn.
It was Naunie's Birthday and our six-month wedding anniversary party. I got Naunie a copy of the book, *The Air Force Wife*.

4 October 1954:
Military Leave. I'm escorting Naunie back to Georgia after her extended one month visit to "The Goose." We got a hop on an RCAF (Royal Canadian Air Force) transport to Montreal. We played Bridge with the RCAF Wing Commander, Edwards and his wife, Sue, in the Montreal *Indian Room*.

5 October 1954:
From Montreal, we changed to a train trip to Boston. We had an all day ride on the train south through Vermont. The fall colors were radiant, totally thrilling. On our arrival back in Sudbury, Massachusetts, we ate at Paul Ecke's Kaffe Stugga in the evening.

Josh Batchelder

15 October 1954: Charleston Air Force Base, South Carolina.
A major storm, Hurricane Hazel, had just passed through the Carolinas.[20] It did a lot of damage to Naunie's cousins, Reverend Ralph and Wright Cousins, parsonage in Marion, South Carolina.

16 October 1954: Trailways Bus Trip north to Dover AFB, Delaware.
We shared the bus with a football team and their band. Throughout the day, following the storm north, we saw storm debris all around us. Many of the passengers and the bus driver shared their stories about the storm's fury and flooding. At Dover, we changed to a train for New York and Springfield, Massachusetts, near Westover AFB. At Westover we crossed paths with my best man, Woody Ayres, on his way back to Goose, following his visit home to Ocala, Florida. Before heading back to Goose, I visited Mom, Mary, Don, Eunice, and Shawn.

19 October 1954:
Back on the Goose, Robby asks me if I put "a bun in the oven" during Naunie's month-long visit to the Degink Hotel.

21 October 1954: Day Alert Sorties
I completed three good intercepts. It was extensive work with my "hand control" (keeping target painted by hand control knob linked to the directional antenna). Most of the time we were in the soup (clouds).

Twelve

The Little Theatre

24 October 1954:
Sunday reading, *The Origins of Wit and Humor*. Wit equals concrete to abstract, whereas, humor is abstract to concrete. Captain Puckett, our squadron Intelligence Officer, shared with me his books on public speaking and unpopular essays.

25 October 1954:
Monday Leadership School – two weeks duration.

31 October 1954:
Reading *Current Tendencies* by philosopher, Betrand Russell. He covered classical, evolutionary, and the scientific spirit of indifference.

1 November 1954:
Movie, "The Best Years of Our Lives".

6 November 1954:
At Saturday midday O-Club meeting, everyone spoke on issues of the Club's operation, Bob Canup, Shorty and Woody Ayres, myself and a couple of captains all put in their two cents worth. That evening at nine, the dance band played and we began dancing. The 59th was swinging again 'til midnight.

Josh Batchelder

12 November 1954:

    Friday, I read, *How To Tell If You're Psychic*. Reverend Alson Smith's book covers parapsychology studies at Harvard, Duke, and City College, New York. About immortality, the scientific evidence sums up a general belief in "the survival of some part of the human spirit after death."

13 November 1954:

    I'm reading, *Cybernetics*, by Wiley and Wiener. At the Base theatre I viewed "Shield for Murder."

14 November 1954:

    I read Alan Barth's, *The Loyalty of Free Man*. On the Canadian side of Goose, I visited the Theatre Workshop. George K, Leona, Woody (Ayers), Stephen, Earnie, and Roy, all went. Miss Billy Murray speaks of her group of five girls and five boys, and their talent. Without an explanation, Bob Richmond walked out. Was he bored or just upset for not receiving more attention?

17 November 1954:

    Evening Meeting of Little Theatre Group. George Kennedy, George Wilson, Bob Turner, Mimi Ferguson, and others have lively discussion about workshop factions. Will we have a plain workshop or a polished play production? M. Wilson had former professional experience in Seattle and England.

18 November 1954: Flight to Torbay, Newfoundland.

    I logged 2+20. Pappy Brims, Milo, Shorty Fuller, and I went to the Torbay O-Club. In French, we joked with our waitress about going to bed with her, "Voulez-vous coucher avec moi, ce soir?"

19 November 1954: Little Theatre Group Meeting.

    Ms. Cox, Leona Ferguson, George Kennedy, Woody, and I discuss one-act plays, radio, songs, sketches, and poems as forms of entertainment.

Black Watch Diary

20 November 1954: The Base Chapel wedding of Tom and Ethel Wright.

They had a beautiful ceremony. I grasped the irony and futility of the limited opportunity for the remaining girls at Goose Bay. One such sweet one, Barbara, told me of her boyfriend, "He's on leave, to his home in New York City. He has a different attitude toward marriage and morals. I try to behave right." She's from a small town. Later, I saw the movie, "Tonight's the Night." It had an Irish setting and starred Barry Fitzgerald, David Niven, and Yvonne DeCarlo.

21 November 1954: Sunday, Theatre Workshop (TW).

Our meeting lasted two and one half hours. Present: Leona, George W., George K, Woody, Bob, and myself. After 35 minutes George W. walked out. Minutes later "Theatre Workshop" was agreed upon as suggested by Bob. It was unanimous. Newcomers to TW: Roy Jackson, an English player/actor and Carl Smidth, dancing work, etc. with Don Dugosh. I'm to get space for Tuesday night's meeting.

22 November 1954: Monday, Service Club TW Meeting.

I flew a round robin (out and back) flight to Harmon AFB, Newfoundland. That evening I attended a TW meeting. We read, *Robespierre*. Gail Knapp and Sherry Canning joined TW. Monologue "Sex is Everything" read by Winnie Weeks, written by Florence Ryerson and Colin Clements.

23 November 1954: Night Alert Duty.

In the middle of my reading, *Strategy in Business, Poker and War*, the Scramble alarm bell sounded. We had a difficult head-on approach to ID a bogey. Three and one-half miles away, my radar screen painted the bogey.[21] I estimated a 700 knot closure rate. We had some sixty to seventy seconds to do a 180 degree turn and execute the maneuver to come close enough to see and radio the aircraft type and tail number to GCI. Later, Bill Taylor (the pilot) asked, "How do you feel when you're in the back seat and nothing is going on, and your pilot is maneuvering around at a very low altitude?" I answered, "I have some uneasiness about our having sufficient clearance to avoid striking hills."

Josh Batchelder

25 November 1954: TW Meeting 2:30 p.m.
   Present: Woody, Sherry, Leona, George, Miss Lucy Cox, Steve, Roy and I. Our decision, "Pot 'Pouri" will be a variety show. We ate Thanksgiving dinner together. We need an emcee for the Christmas show. We talked about doing "A Christmas Carol" by Charles Dickens, or, a monologue of "The Three Lovers" by Will Carlton. Maybe, "The Women" by Rudyard Kipling. George, Woody, and I had tea at Leona's afterwards.

26 November 1954:
   I read, *Air Power: Key to Survival* by Major Alexander deSeversky. I copied in my diary, The Rubaiyat by Omar Khayyam:

>   "Oh threats of Hell and Hopes of Paradise!
>   One thing, at least is certain – this life flies.
>   One thing is certain and the rest is lies.
>   The flower that once has blown forever dies.
>   Waste not your hours, nor in vain pursuit
>   Of this and that endeavor and dispute;
>   Better be joined with the fruitful grape
>   Than sadder after none, or bitter fruit."

28 November 1954: TW Meeting.
   Ernest Scarborough, having worked at an Oregon radio station, talked about a Philharmonic production of "Kiss Me Kate" and about when Stan Kenton did a guest show spot at Geiger AFB, Washington. Later this evening when I returned to the barracks, my buddies continued ribbing me about my theatre connection.

Thirteen

The Bob Hope Show

29 November 1954, 1:45 AM:
   Phil Gereau got us out of bed and told us that "Pa Kettle" (Leonard) and Woody (Ayres) had crashed on a GCA final (approach to field). Al and I went down to the flight line to take over alert duty. Major Davidson, CO, was there. In a helicopter, Pappy Brims and Robby went to the scene. It was dark. They saw flashlights and a bonfire.

29 November 1954:
   At daybreak, by helicopter, Pa and Woody were picked up. They suffered minor injuries. At our squadron meeting, Colonel Stoney spoke about traffic control history, the present day set-up and future trends.

30 November 1954: 8:30 p.m. TW meeting, Service Club.
   We began casting. Woody mentioned that he might start a diary. Then he said, "But, I don't wish to become a Boswell." During an inventory (assignment) of the PX Warehouse (Post Exchange) we counted stacks of boxes holding beer mugs. For their handles, they had figurines of big breasted girls. After two cases of them sold like hot cakes, they were banned from being sold at the BX. Could our would-be Baptist Minister, Col. J. B. Knapp have stopped the sales?

1 December 1954:
   I met Lt. Eddie Knight. Nine months ago, while he was in flight training at Bradford, Florida, he met and married a girl from Miami. Now, he's flying F-86s. He's bound for six months duty in France.

3 December 1954:
   I read *Semantic Difficulties in International Communication* by Edmund S. Glenn. It was all about patterns of thought and thinking classifications.

Josh Batchelder

4 December 1954: O-Club Caribou Room.

Eddie Knight and I met again. We talked about the F-86s unique and unforgiving landing problems. We talked further about the ineptness of a certain control tower operator. Finally we expressed worries about the limited amount of instrument flying time of many new pilots. For example, the hazards facing day-fighter pilots visiting the Goose and trying to land during adverse weather conditions.

7-11 December 1954 - TW Shows:
"A Christmas Carol" production.

12 December 1954: Sunday - TW Meeting.

Jim (from Canadian side, RCAF) becomes responsible for Xmas caroling and talent show.

13 December 1954: O-Club - Our Flight Party.

Major Stein was present. It was a quiet meeting. In our renovated Club, the combo played nostalgic music. Curt Stegner got a kick out of my remarking about my RN mother's repeated observation that, "Your feet and hands grow first; and then they stop growing at 18." When mine kept growing beyond 19, she didn't know what to say. The new signs in the O-Club irritated us. For example, *Mess attendants only, may relocate furniture, and 252 maximum people in this Ballroom, only; by order of the Base Commander, Colonel J. B. Knapp.*

14 December 1954, Night Duty: Combat Air Patrol (CAP).

Al and I spotted a very high speed blinking object estimated to be flying about 10,000 feet above us. It was going in the opposite direction from us. We estimated its airspeed at 1,500 to 2,000 knots. Was it a flying saucer?[22]

16 December 1954: O-Club Evening.

Eddie Knight spoke about his all-night date in Las Vegas, "We had a few drinks. I spent fifty bucks. I didn't even get a kiss."

Black Watch Diary

17 December 1954: Eight F-89Ds arrived.

All of our flight crews were seeking a chance to ferry the F-94 *Starfires* back to the Lockheed Base at Ontario, California. Major Davidson said, "There will be two crews from the 59th and two from the 74th FIS from Thule." He had just returned from our Wing Commander's Call. He reported that General Barcus said, "I spend seventy percent of my time trying to put out the fires. Last year alone, our wing aircraft accidents and incidents physical damages cost Uncle Sam over $4,000,000." ($32,000,000 in today's dollars).

19 December 1954: TW Meeting at the Base Schoolhouse.

The first casting of "Hayfever" took place. Stan, Jim, Nell, Jackie, Leona and Woody had parts. I got the part of Richard, the "Diplomatist."

20 December 1954: Day Alert and evening at TW.

Initially we met at Bob and Rosie Reid's place on the Canadian side of Goose. Bob and Rosie are from New Brunswick, Canada. Chico Brindle said, "I'll try to get Spaniards, with guitars, to sing for us." Jackie Gould said, "I'll find a girl to sing." After the meeting, we went to the meeting room at the Base Hospital to practice.

25 December 1954: O-Club Christmas Dinner.

We had a good Christmas dinner around a big table that had Captains Hays and Brims families, plus Saylor, Komp, Phil, Al, Harrington, and I. That evening the party continued at Captain Hays' place. He and John Komp both married girls from China. We danced and sang, borrowing the few visiting wives of our comrades along with the single girls from the barracks across the street from the O-Club.

26 December 1954: Canadian Side of Goose.

Our TW practiced "Hayfever." We heard that Jackie and Chico made out. It was an "accident." Ernie and others handed out bits of advice. Ernie had the most to say!

27 December 1954: Night Alert.

It was my first Scramble in the last three weeks. We completed several intercepts. Because of the lower level jet-stream over the CADIZ, the bogies were

Josh Batchelder

way off their filed ETA's for entering the coastal CADIZ Zone.

28 December 1954: RCAF Reception.
Group Captain Ball hosted his reception at the Canadian O-Club. I met Flying Officers Willis, Rhodes, Reid, and their wives. The Canadian officers were lucky to have family quarters. Rosie, Bob Reid's wife, was shining. Squadron Leader Cummings was there. Later in the afternoon the University of Washington chorus visited our flight line.

29 December 1954: Base Joint Communications Conference.
For the USAF, Lt. Colonel Storey presided. Squadron Leader West represented the RCAF. Mr. O'Neal, the Base Communications Officer, along with Majors Bass and Prygan, were at the blackboard. They discussed all aspects of the effects of weather on Teletype, RAPCON (Radar Approach Control), and Flight Plan Operations.

30-31 December 1954: Bob Hope Show.
Work was underway in flight line hangar seven to build the setting and stage for the Bob Hope Show. Because of my work on the show committee I was assigned a personal vehicle. The stage drop was completed with the help of SAC Liaison, Col. Griffin. Mimi introduced me to Mr. White, Hangar #7 Electronics Chief. Warrant Officer James and A/2C Barger, from the Parachute Shop prepared the big banner that was hung across the stage. It read, "*WHEN THE DUCKS WALK AT GOOSE, WE FLY!*" The Base Communication Shop set up the sound system. Mohnesen, Drake, and Meritt were from the Base Machine Shop. Sergeants Bowman and Stoudt came from the Base Photo Lab. Mr. Henry Le Blanc assisted us from the AIO Workshops.

1 January 1955: The Bob Hope Show went on.
My Alert Duty had priority. I missed witnessing a great New Year's Day show at *The Goose*. I heard that actors Bill Holden and Brenda Marshall performed along with the gorgeous actress Anita Eckburg. Maggie Whiting sang, "God Bless America," and "White Christmas." Jerry Colona, comedian, hammed-it-up with Bob. Bob, as always, had a long list of good jokes with beautiful babes all around him.

Fourteen

"You No Survive, You Dead"

11 January 1955:

At our Arctic Survival School, Captain Hinkson gave us detailed instructions for wording messages: Short, clear, single meaning words. They should be large enough to be read by air rescue scanners. I remembered the last June summer survival course statement by Major Knutson, "You no survive, you dead!" Avoid words that have double meaning, like GEM. Show each letter, use words with one phonetic value. No silent words like GNAT, KNIT.

12 January 1955: More Survival Theory.

Doug A. was assigned as our third tepee mate. He's from Harmon. He was an "old" WWII RO. He flew fifty-five missions in the *Black Widow* P-61 and P-70 in the ETO (European Theatre) WWII.[23] The Black Widow saw its first combat on D-Day, June 6, 1944.

13 January 1955: 0900 Hours.

We were loaded onto trucks and dropped off on a hillside near Pinetree GCI.

Black Widow P-61

Josh Batchelder

Sporting snowshoes and packs, we tracked two and one half nautical miles across a string of four frozen solid lakes. When we arrived at our campsite, we learned that Sgt. Skrettingen would be our instructor. He was an old woodsman from Wyoming. He has responsibility for aircrews nine through twelve. We built our teepee.

14 January 1955: Labrador Outback.

Under the watchful guidance of Sgt. Skrettingen, we began setting out snares. During our trek to our camp site, we didn't spot any animals. We did, however, hear more detail on words to use when constructing messages in the snow. They must be easily spotted and understood by airborne search and rescue teams, like "need food" or "look west." Sarge said, "You guys know by now that the reddish orange color on your personal equipment and aircraft make it easy for searchers to spot you when you are down in the white snow."

15 January 1955: Survival Signals Training.

We're learning all the time. With birch bark and spruce limbs, we constructed a spruce torch. After dark, we lit the torch. During the day we improved our campsite. Visiting Dee Wilson and Nick Stone's teepee, we learned that their third occupant, Oscar, had a father who was a lumberjack. They said, "Oscar's good, at least for chopping wood." At the end of their scramble sorties, our 59th buddies *buzzed* our site. Due to a bad camera setting, Al fretted about not having all of his treasured survival training pictures.

16 January 1955: Major Willie Knutson's Campsite.

We chased a squirrel, only to learn that it was Captain Hinkson's pet; it hung around his cabin. This is our last night in the boonies. It's been really easy. We could have had to endure below zero weather. Instead, we lucked into a January thaw for our in-the-field training.

17 January 1955: End of Survival Training.

In thick snow slush, we jogged two and one half miles back to our waiting truck for Goose.

Black Watch Diary

Josh Batchelder, Doug A., and Al Kramer
Arctic Survival School

Josh and Al in their teepee

Don Rogers shared his survival story... "*After a day or two of classroom instruction, we teamed up in groups of two (pilot and radar operator in F-94 aircrew cases). We were given a survival kit, bedroll, small tarp, parachute, mess kit, ice saw and small single shot .22 rifle, like we carried in our survival kits when we flew. Then they gave us snowshoes, showed us how to walk in them and the class began walking west into the "wilds" of early December Labrador. There was three or four feet of snow on the ground. We walked an hour or hour and a half in our show shoes with our packs on our backs. The instructors had a dog sled. One of the students in the class was a Captain from Brooklyn, NY. He had probably never been camping in his life and couldn't or wouldn't do anything for himself. His partner was a little better.*

"*The first thing we did when we got to our campsite was pack down the snow in the area we were going to erect our parachute tent and build a fire. The temperature was warm for that time of the year. It was below freezing, but not much. Our team, two guys from Mississippi and Texas who had spent time in the open and camped out many times before, had no problem. We had our tent up, had cut wood and had our fire started and the team with the Brooklyn Captain, who flew the Base C-47, didn't have their tent up, fire made or anything. Joe and I helped, no, that is incorrect, we erected their tent and built their fire. We made them cut their own wood. We stayed out two nights and walked back on the third day. On the way back to the base, the Brooklyn Captain and his buddy lagged way behind everyone else and we had to stop frequently for them to catch up, as the instructors were afraid they would lose sight of us and get lost. I honestly think these two would have NOT survived if they had ever gone down and had to use this training.*"

Fifteen
Be A Panther, Not a Tiger

Life Is A Tragedy For Those Who Feel, And A Comedy For Those Who Think.
—Horace Walpole (1717-1797)

19 January 1955: Day Alert Sorties.
    Curt Stegner and I flew two Scramble Sorties. We intercepted an SA-16 (search and rescue seaplane), and a KC-97 *Tanker* from Harmon. Curt informed me that on January 28th he would be marrying Winnie McMullen. She'll be his beautiful Canadian bride.

20 January 1955: 59th Squadron Communications Shop.
    I spent most of the day at my Comm Shop. It's my secondary duty assignment. I reviewed the CEI (Communications Electronics Instruments) files. In the early evening I attended practice with my Little Theatre Group. Later, in my room, I read Thomas Carlyle. I wrote in my diary, "Our main business is not to see what lies dimly at a distance, but to do what lies clearly, at hand."

21 January 1955: Comm Shop.
    More CEI activity at the Comm Shop. I inventoried our records. Later, at the Base library, I read more of *General Semantics*. I entered in my diary: *Experience is never at fault; it is only our judgment that is in error…wrongly, do we cry out against experience.*

22 January 1955: O-Club Dance.
    We had a formal dance. There was much noise and joking about the fire marshal's complaints about our barracks buddies safety consciousness. Plenty of boisterous songs were sung.

Black Watch Diary

25 January 1955: Early Morning Sortie.
Al and I flew a sunrise sortie and marvelled at the beautiful, cold clear blue skies and snow covered countryside. We completed four intercepts. Winging our way back to the Base, we paid our respects to our buddies in the boonies survival school. They were camped on the iced-over lake. We gave them a better buzz job than their low pass over our survival training camp, when we dropped down to a few feet above the ice. At 400 mph, I was uneasy. I thought we would scrape the ice. Over their camp, we did a sharp pull-up and lit our Afterburner. Our AB blast shock waves nearly blew over their teepees and tents.

27 January 1955: Staff Meeting - Little Theatre Workshop.
Major Prarat led our staff meeting. Major Davidson was introduced to give us a debriefing of his inspection. He said, "I was sent by the 64th Air Division to look over your flight operations." He detailed some tough comments. Later, I attended Curt Stegner's stag party. After the 59th critique, I felt I needed an extra drink.

28 January 1955: Day-Alert.
With no scramble alarms, it was a quiet day. I read *How to Make Common Sense* by Flesch, and *Becoming a Winner*, by Dorothea Brande. Late afternoon I went to the wedding of Curt and Winnie. Their reception was in the Caribou Room of the O-Club.

Goose Bay Air Field Chapel

Josh Batchelder

30 January 1955: Theatre Workshop, Base Service Club.
 Because of an O-Club scheduling mix-up, we were bumped from our reservation by the higher priority given our visiting Harmon SAC refueling squadron. It was a reminder to me that because of the Cold War, General Curt LeMay, SAC Commander, controlled everything.[24] The Sunday evening Service Club atmosphere was dead.

2 February 1955: 59th Communication Shop.
 We worked on installing equipment. Gil and I completed a letter to Major Prarat, CO, about the Communication Shop's lack of personnel and experience.

5 February 1955: Night-Alert Duty.
 At 10 p.m., Dave White with RO Burt Tillet returned from his Scramble Sortie (four active-air intercepts). Dave decided to buzz the Saturday night Scramble Inn party at our barracks.[25] On a course parallel to the BOQ, at about 90 feet, he struck a 100-foot-high unlighted radio tower. His accelerated speed (AB ignited?) shot him up to 4,000 feet where he had to orbit for a couple of minutes waiting for a Pan Am DC7 to land. The engine continued to produce power and landing was tense but uneventful, with no personal injuries. The *Starfire's* underside was gashed from the tower strike. The radome had blown off and half the nose gear support had been cut through. There were a couple of other unlighted towers in the vicinity (about half a mile from the BOQ) and they were all removed in the next few days. Naturally, Dave had some hoops to go through in the next few months, but after all settled down he left the service."[26]

9 February 1955: Four fatalities from Lake Melville accident.
 First Lieutenants Curt Stegner and RO Al Culpepper's bird collided with Second Lieutenants Don 'Pa Kettle' Leonard and RO John C. Sheperd's, bird. The accident report said that, "Aircraft debris was spread over a mile across the ice on Lake Melville." The collision happened three nautical miles (NM) East of Rabbit Island. The weather was the likely cause. Snow flurries and the late morning sun shining through caused the blinding white-out conditions. The temperature was minus 9 degrees Fahrenheit. Curt and Winnie enjoyed only thirteen days of married life. For flight pay, Curt was getting his flight time in before rotating back to the States with

Black Watch Diary

Damage to Dave White's Plane

Radio Towers

Josh Batchelder

Winnie. It was reported that Don and Curt had been practicing intercepts using their IFF-capable radar scopes. Their equipment likely failed.

Dave White gave me his rewrite of the fatal aircraft accident, "For some reason I recall they were coming in, in formation as a flight of two, for a straight-in instrument landing over the Lake Melville ice. As they flew under the overcast they could see the runway, but the low visibility obscured the horizon and the theory was that Curt went visual (ended his instrument approach), got too low and flew into the ice, taking Don (Don's aircraft) with him.

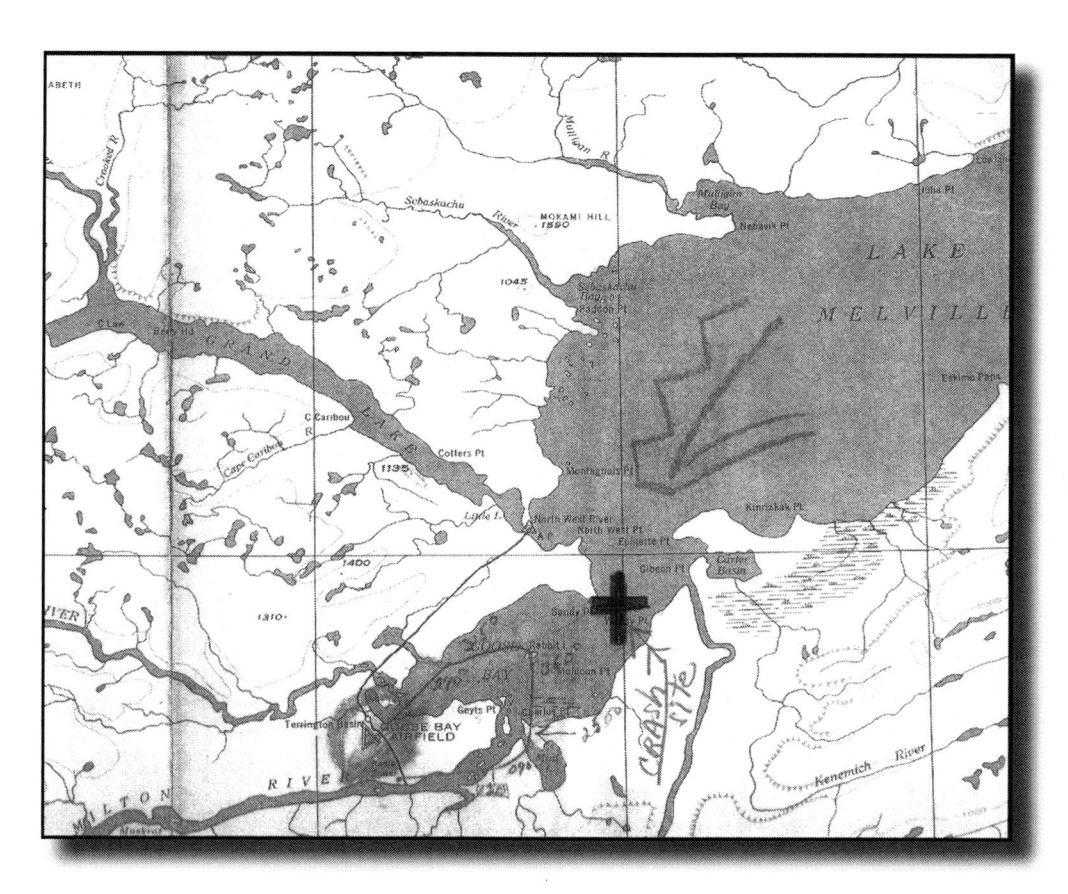

Map of the Crash Site

Black Watch Diary

9 February 1955, Afternoon: The 64th Air Division Inspectors Visit.

As a result of the accident, Lt. Colonel Weaver, Major McCawthen, and Captain Bliss of the 64th descended upon us.

10 February 1955: Communication Section Inspection.

Lt./Colonel Mitchel asked me about Sgt. Graybill's communication equipment clearance of the write-ups on the two aircraft involved in the accident, numbered 871 and 510. Graybill had signed-off the write-ups as "ground-checked OK."[27] General Barcus arrived from Thule Air Base. He was on Base for an hour and a half. It was long enough to fire, on-the-spot, Major Prarat. He became our new 59th Executive Officer. The General berated our Flight Commanders saying, "You're running a half-assed squadron…like a bunch of CAP (Civil Air Patrol) members, maybe worse."

11 February 1955: 0800 hours, 64th Air Division Visit.

Colonel Meyer, from the 64th, spoke to us. "You need to be panthers, not tigers. What I mean is, you must be more cunning and courageous…be more responsible…allow more margin for safety." Lt. Colonel Victor Walton is now the Fourth Squadron Commander that has been assigned to us since I arrived last May. Colonel Meyer went on to say, "I brought the boys down to help Major Prarat out. I want to stop the 59th's trend of eleven flying accidents in one year."

12 February 1955: 59th Squadron Meeting, 0800 hours.

This was the fourth day of meetings about our major accidents. Our new CO, Lt./Colonel Walton, began, "I've had four outfits…I know how we can work together and cooperate, up and down the line." I felt like a problem was found and solved for me without my realizing that it had been a problem! That is, like sin being pointed out to an ignorant native, who never realized that such a moral issue existed, before being told as much.

13-15 February 1955: Theatre Workshop Meetings.

During the day, I forwarded to Pepperill AFB the *classified* documents relating to our accidents. In the evenings for our upcoming talent show, at the Base Service Club, our Little Theatre Group had daily planning and practice.

Josh Batchelder

20 February 1955: Flying, Comm Shop, and Reading.

In the morning, in the Base Air Rescue Squadron's *Albatross* (seaplane) I logged two hours of VO (Visual Observer) time. The AC pilot was Captain Jim Plank. His Co-pilot was Captain Wise. Captain Plank told me he was originally an "old" Connally AFB Airman. My Comm Shop men put up a new antenna atop our Alert Hangar. I read, *The Protestant Primer on Roman Catholicism* and *The Mind Alive* by Harry Overstreet.

21 February 1955: Labrador Coast, Live Rocket Firing.

For practice, on my first F89D *Scorpion* practice flight over water, we fired our rockets at a target. I received orders for my next duty station, Paine Field, Everett, Washington, just north of Seattle, bordering Puget Sound. I spoke with RCAF (Royal Canadian Air Force) Wing Commander Grant about supporting our Theatre Workshop for our upcoming talent show. Commander Grant gave us one hundred dollars.

22 February 1955:

Staff Sergeant Stuart, our Talent Show Director, met with our motley group for the first dress rehearsal. We saw enough to decide to quit "Hayfever" and merge the two Base play groups. Our Flight Commanders, Captains Goodnow and Patrick, had fun kidding me about my play group activity.

Colonel Knapp

Sixteen

Arctic Doldrums

26 February 1955: Saturday evening.
　　The January thaw has long since passed. We've returned to cold weather and heavy snow accumulation. Inside the O-Club our troops drank, danced, and sang. I dimmed the ballroom lights. Soon, Colonel Knapp turned them back up. He came over to our corner of the club and asked me, "Why did you go against my wishes and turn the lights down?" I didn't have a good answer. The cat and mouse game continued.

　　Our Intel Officer, Captain Puckett is half Indian. He likes to drink. He enjoys himself. On occasions, like this evening, he has appeared to make lewd moves on the dance floor. His carefree spirit has earned him the title of *Fuck-it Puckett*. Tonight, about mid-night, the dance music stopped. Club members "poured" out the doors. Colonel and Mrs. Knapp appeared unsteady as they exited the Club. By the door, Mrs. Knapp fell into a deep snow bank. Who would come to her rescue? None other than Captain *Fuck-it Puckett*. I'm reading, *Do Gestures Speak Louder Than Words?* by Birdenhistel, PhD.

7 March 1955:
　　About noon, I talked with CO Colonel Walton. We exchanged views about current attitudes and changes in the military. We bantered and chuckled over the rationalizations that are often needed to deal with the challenges and behavior of men at war. He suggested I read *Lee's Lieutenants*. I'm sure he was thinking about General Barcus, Colonel Meyer, and Colonel Jordan's visit from the 33rd Wing, following our rash of accidents, and the need to effect change in our flight crews' attitudes and behavior.

Josh Batchelder

11 March 1955:

I flew a scramble sortie with Dee Wilson. There was a mean fifty-five knot (63 mph) seventy degree crosswind. Our approach and landing was a real challenge. At Goose we have no nearby alternate landing sites.

14 March 1955:

Captain Almon, along with two other officers, delivered his *mia culpa* talk at our Ops Meeting. Because of his failure to comply with procedures (Article Seven, Item Three, etc.), he nearly got an armed ejection seat in his face.[28] Even though he had 4700 hours of jet time, his mistake could have killed him. The lesson, "We need a new attitude and concept for flying safety. Whenever we're on the ground around aircraft, not just in the air…we must go back to basics and pay attention to procedures and precautions."

17 March 1955:

I'm reading, *The Path of Buddhism – Life's Four Noble Truths:*
A. Suffering is universal
B. The cause of suffering is craving
C. The cure, elimination of craving
D. The way of eliminating craving is following the middle way, an eight-fold path:
    1. Right knowledge
    2. Right intention
    3. Right speech
    4. Right conduct
    5. Right means of livelihood
    6. Right effort
    7. Right mindfulness
    8. Right concentration

The partial code of conduct:
    1. Abstain from taking life
    2. Abstain from taking what's not given
    3. Abstain from illegal sexual pleasures
    4. Abstain from lying
    5. Abstain from intoxicants which can cloud the mind

Black Watch Diary

18 March 1955:

I read fifty pages of *They Called Him Stonewall*. This book is all about character guidance that our CO recommended. I picked up moccasins for Naunie at the Hudson Bay store. Later I reflected on my career opportunity in the Air Force. I'm learning it could mean being away from Naunie for long periods. Being separated isn't good for our marriage or right for any two in love. I'll appreciate her more and more especially when I return (from Goose). Reading Will Rogers, *Ambassador of Good Will*; *The Prince of Wit and Wisdom* by P. J. O'Brien.

Arctic Doldrums

Seventeen

Escaping Goose

19 March 1955:
A crew chief drove his jeep into our bird's tip-tank, delaying our first leg of the flight to the Lockheed Plant, Ontario, California. Pappy Brims gave him a stern lecture.

20 March 1955, 1120 hours:
Our tip-tank repaired, Al and I departed Goose for Presque Isle, Maine. Cloudy, rainy weather and extended holding for our GCA (Ground Control Approach) exhausted our fuel. We declared "minimum fuel" to traffic control, and were cleared to GCA for immediate landing. We touched down with zero gallons indicated. Our engine quit on the roll-out at the end of the runway. Phew! We had to be towed to the parking ramp. We logged two hours and twenty minutes. At the O-Club I bumped into Harry Creech, Bob Betts, Renshaw, Chuck Sammut and Sims, all buddies from Connally. We caught up on all the happenings since Cadet Training. The accidents, assignments, and Chuck's marriage. Chuck was a roommate with me and two others at Ellington AFB, Houston. Later we saw a movie, "The Long Gray Line." It was about West Point.

21 March 1955:
I saw more of the troops I'd known at Connally, including Frank Powders. He is in a theatre group at Presque Isle. Clay Wilkins is on his way to Pilot Training. In town, we ate at the Northeastland Hotel. I picked up a book, *A Treasury of Wit and Wisdom*, to read later.

22 March 1955:
Lousy weather at Westover AFB, Massachusetts, held us up from leaving

Black Watch Diary

Presque Isle. Evening talk with Woody Halter and learned about his experiences the past year at Iceland and Presque Isle.

23 March 1955: Presque Isle O-Club.

Weather delayed our departure for Westover Field. We played Bingo and spent more time talking with Clay Wilkins and Woody Halter and his date. Began reading *The Conquest of Happiness*, by Bertrand Russell. Base alert for six hours today.

24 March 1955: Westover Field.

En route to Westover, strong easterly winds blew us fifteen miles west of our intended route. We were under the IFR control of Eaglebeak and then Wild Bill traffic control centers. Upon landing at Westover I called Mother and Donald at Sudbury. Also, I called Naunie to tell her I expected to come to Atlanta for overnight at Dobbins Air Force Base, Marietta, Georgia.

26 March 1955: Dover AFB, Delaware.

Because of weather again, our flight plan was changed to a layover at Dover AFB. I thought about the naming of our children this morning. We need to do this together so that I'll feel more a part of our children. I miss Naunie terribly. This evening I am very anxious to see her tomorrow.

27 March 1955, Sunday:

It's our first anniversary. Because of an unfavorable 170 knot lower level jet stream head wind, Al and I are still stuck at Dover. I called my honey in the afternoon and was glad to hear she'd played Bridge with Jean McGee, wife of my squadron comrade at Goose. I finished reading *The Conquest of Happiness*. When I saw Captain Andy Veelander, he asked about his girlfriend, Marie, back on the Goose. I told him that I didn't notice any one in particular going out with his *milk maid*.

29 March 1955: Dobbin AFB, Marietta at 5:30 a.m.

We finally arrived in Atlanta. I called our cousin Boozer Payne's place in Atlanta. Honey answered the phone. Thirty minutes later she arrived at Dobbins

Josh Batchelder

AFB Operations, along with Boozer, Annie, Boozer Jr., and Keith Payne to see us during our short refueling stop. Honey, over eight months pregnant, is beginning to really pop out with our child. It's like the cute young girl figurine's belly popping with *Kilroy Was Here!* stamped across it. Jean McGee and her family plus my honey and the Paynes' watched our 1320 hours take-off.

30 March 1955: Perrin AFB, Northern Texas.

After a refueling stop at Navy Memphis, we arrived at Perrin about 1615 hours. We were out of oxygen. Before we dropped down to a lower altitude, we noticed that we were quite *tired* from the lack of oxygen.

1 April 1955: Perrin AFB, Texas.

Awaiting favorable winds for our flight to Roswell AFB, New Mexico, I read an article "On the Land of Confucius." Confucianism is defined as rational, orderly, matter-of-fact, and humanistic. Taoism is known to be more romantic, intuitive, vague, and mystical. Entered much description in my diary, including Yin and Yang and how they differ. Taoism followers look to nature in troubled times; whereas followers of Confucianism look within themselves. Spoke with Barbara about children. She definitely doesn't want more. She dislikes people around her when she's pregnant. She wants to 'call the shots.' Her child wasn't planned.

2 April 1955: Roswell AFB, New Mexico.

We arrived in very high cross winds in the middle of a dust storm. In partial obscuration, we did an overhead visual approach for landing. For a few seconds after the break, the dust prevented us from seeing the long parallel runways. Continuing to circle around to the final for landing, we saw the end of the runway clear up. We continued on and landed. After landing, we discovered that the high cross winds had blown us off course a mile from our intended runway.

3 April 1955: Roswell, AFB, New Mexico.

At take off, just before braking ground, we had to abort and return to operations. In addition to a vicious left cross wind condition we had a high left wing strut. This caused us to nearly cartwheel off the runway. With a blistered tire, we recovered at the end of the runway. Pappy (Brims), in our companion flight of four, also returned to the Ops parking ramp and tied down. Due to the high and gusty wind conditions Maggie and Bill went on to El Paso International, instead of Biggs AFB.

4 April 1955: Ontario International Airport.

We had an 8:20 a.m. departure from Roswell AFB; then, we stopped to refuel at "Willey" (William AFB, Arizona). Enroute, we flew over Fort Apache AP which was near a 10,000 foot high plateau. Next, we passed Desert Island AP. We "sold" our bird (a legal form changing responsibility). After a two and a half hour wait for the Base transportation driver to find us, we got to the Biltmore Hotel, Los Angeles. Because of weather and maintenance, it took us sixteen days to ferry our F94 back to the States and turn it over to Lockheed. It would probably later be delivered to a National Guard Reserve Squadron.

5 April 1955: Los Angeles.

We connected with our flight buddies at the hotel as they completed selling their 94s. We stood at Hollywood and Vine for awhile. We ate lunch at Clifton's. Sal doesn't like the place, Al does. Sal said, "It's too foreign. It gives me the creeps!" When I said, "I think they shame people into paying full price for food," he remarked, "Josh, ya don't believe in people."

6 April 1955: Chicago, Illinois Airport.

Sal's mother picked us up at the airport and fed us a "splendid spaghetti" meal (chicken, pizza, cake, pie, beer). All of Sal's Italian family was there.

9 April 1955:

Back on Goose Air Base after April 7th flight on the United Airlines "milk run" to Hartford, Connecticut and connecting to Westover, we had an engine failure thirty minutes out of Westover. We stopped at Grenier AFB, New Hampshire for a two and a half hour maintenance fix. Finally, we departed Grenier and made it to Goose. Evening at the O-Club, I said goodbye to my comrades and friends. I've had three weeks break from the Goose and tomorrow I'll begin the process of clearing the Base and rotating to the States. Hopefully, I'll have a long enough leave to be with Naunie when she delivers our first child. Then, it's on to Paine AFB, Washington, North of Seattle.[29]

Eighteen

FIGMO[30], Time To Go

10-14 April 1955:

I've got my orders, FIGMO, I've begun clearing Goose. The first order of business was to turn in my heavy personal flight equipment. Later, I hung around the O-Club for more goodbyes. 10 April: I heard about RO, Brad Webster's fatal crash into the Bay at Harmon Air Base (Newfoundland). 11 April: I helped Phil Gereau with packing his baggage for shipment. Next, I transferred my responsibilities of the Comm Shop to a new chief. Then, I turned in my paperwork to finance for per diem reimbursement of the California trip expenses. 12 April: The last paperwork was Squadron clearance. Woody Ayers and I talked about his decision to get off active duty and complete his education at the University of Chicago. This evening I went to my TW meeting. They're thinking about a "Traveling Show Boat," a variety program. Jack Livingstone gave this idea a big push. 13 April 1955: Awaiting a MATS flight Southbound, I'm reading Bernard Baruch's *A Philosophy for Our Times*. I went over to the Base Library where Maris P. Saunders, Librarian, wrote in my diary from Hemingway's *Men at War*, "Learning to suspend your imagination and live completely in the very second of the present minute with no before and no after is the greatest gift a soldier (airmen) can acquire." I completed my income tax returns and bought American Express Travelers Checks.

15 April 1955:

I missed one morning hop to Westover AFB. I finally got out of Goose and arrived at Westover. While I was waiting the MATS hop I saw RO Woody leaving to ferry another 94B to Lockheed, Ontario California via Limestone AFB, Maine, then Westover AFB and continuing Westward.

Black Watch Diary

16 April 1955: Charleston, AFB, South Carolina.
Navy Petty Officer Twilliger overheard my phone call attempt to catch a scheduled Greyhound bus headed north. He volunteered to drive me the nine miles to the bus station to catch the Athens, Georgia Express. At 7:30 p.m. Honey was at the station to drive me to Elberton.

18 April 1955: Elberton, Georgia.
Honey took me to town to get two outfits for my birthday, the day after tomorrow.

20 April 1955:
Miz Gladys made me a Japanese fruit cake for my birthday. We're awaiting our first child due in several weeks.

25 April 1955:
Reading, *The Universe and Dr. Einstein* by Lincoln Burnett.

26-30 April 1955:
I'm organizing and planning my future, by getting my records together and inquiring about an ROTC Instructor's position for when I separate from service next March. We went to get a check-up for Honey. Mary Dean Vandiver was at the hospital with Lexa and Fred. At the Elberton Theatre we saw "Dr. Jekyll and Mr. Hyde." At the show we saw Naunie's friends, Ingrid and Shirley. During this period I traveled to Washington, DC and Maxwell AFB, Montgomery, Alabama to explore more options for my work and study next year.

6-15 May 1955:
Awaiting the birth of our baby and family activities: We went down to the river with Honey's family, including Buck, Betsy, Starke Jaudon, Mister Bob, Miz Gladys, and friends, Mary Dean, and Lee Harrell. Playing Gin Rummy, Bridge, Hearts and Indian Dice. We while away the time awaiting the birth of our child.

Josh Batchelder

23-28 May 1955:
Our baby isn't here yet. I must get on the road to report for duty to Paine Field. Over the next several days from Elberton I drove the northern route to Washington State. I arrived on the 28th and reconnected with my buddies. Mac, Bob Estes, Burley Bauer, Bill Taylor, and the others, all friends, had "worked" to get this choice state-side assignment to Washington. Soon, Smitty's wife is about to deliver their little one. Bill Rutherford arrived today (28 May). He said, "Gene Moen is doing well at Minneapolis." Bergstrom said to me, "You've got a good head for the outside, Josh. You shouldn't hesitate to separate."

29-30 May 1955:
With Binnon, I traveled around Everett Washington looking at apartments and homes to rent. As I was writing Honey, she was having Naunie Thiery. She has made me very happy. I proceeded to begin handing out Dutch Master cigars. Smitty, Bergstrom, Johnny J., Kerkson, McCarthy and Burley Bauer all got one.

31 May 1955:
Leaving the 83rd Fighter Operations, I looked back once again to the parked F89D *Scorpions* and the flight line sign:

> **We can beat any man**
> **From any land**
> **At any game**
> **That he can name**
> **For any amount**
> **That he can count.**

Black Watch Diary

Love Affair

By Bob Fritsch, 1954

I have stirred the star filled cauldron of the sky.
Played tag among the thunder clouds
And dodged the lightning bolts from anvil head to anvil head.
I have reached out for the aurora borealis,
Flitting, dancing, beautiful, and tantalizing, teasing, changing,
But always, like a reluctant virgin, just out of reach.
I have been drenched by St. Elmo's fire,
And watched it skip and vibrate and roll along the leading edge of wings
That glowed in eerie spectre light.

I have wandered through the valley's shadow
Bathed in moonlight, turned gossamer by a thin layer of cirrus,
Surrounded by surging battlements of frontal cumulo nimbus,
Their majestic towers rising high above the ethereal plane,
The full moon shining on the solid undercast
Cutting swaths of light, tempting eager feet to tread.
One brief instant of beauty-sheer, unadulterated
Cast upon the brain to remain there forever.

I have watched night creep across the earth,
Watched it's tendrils, like fog, enshroud the countryside.
Watched lights blink on in a thousand farmyards
As the tangible, blanket of darkness, was inexorably pulled across the land
I have danced with moonbeams and gloried in their glow.
Have touched the glowing face of Venus,
Enamored by her beauty, as she shimmers low on the horizon.
Have watched her turn with me, cavort with me,
But always dancing out of reach.

Josh Batchelder

I have seen the sun rise at midnight
Above the cracked, torn, broken face of the great glaciers,
Have watched it set at noon in Sonderstrom Bay
Creating a ghostly city of icebergs of every shape, size and hue.
Icebergs rising from the mist as medieval castles rise along the moor.
Godlike, I have made the sun rise and set a dozen times
In the space of heartbeats.
Soared up above the clouds to watch it rise again,
Then glide down on golden wings to watch it disappear.

I have seen the nighty westward flowing rivers:
The Missouri and the Snake; the Republican and Platte;
Laid out beneath my speeding wings, like a road map to mountain peaks.
I have sped across the plains towards the snow capped spires of the Rockies,
Have flashed low across the golden gate, and buzzed the walls of Alcatraz,
Flaunting my freedom to the poor devils trapped within its walls.
I have winged across the desert and looked up at mountain tops.
I have seen the crater of the sun, and flown the canyon of the Colorado.
I have watched Lake Mead rise out of the desolate baroness
And seen the lights of Vegas glitter like a million jewels.

I have saddled the wind and rode her like a comet
As she whisked me across the sky at breathless pace.
Have seen her, like a vengeful woman scorned, rant, rave, roar, and destroy.
Have known her as a constant faithful lover
Carrying me aloft to dizzying heights of ecstasy,
And felt her fickle wrath as she tossed and buffeted my body
And flung me through the firmament.

I have mourned with saddened heart and smiling face
Those friends who died amidst the flaming wreckage of their craft.
Their bodies battered, broken and burned.
Raised high my glass in silent pledge
Drank long, then dashed it to the wall.
Yes, I have stirred the star filled cauldron of the sky,
And walked the fearful path to danger's door.
I have felt the tickling taste of death in the rarified world above.
Have known the fear of falling and still I am in love.
For always at the last crucial moment, cradled in my silver womb
Have glided safely back to mother earth.

Black Watch Diary

Take Off! F-89D *Scorpions*

Northrop F-89D *Scorpion*

F-94Bs , C-124 Transport in Background

Epilogue/Legacy

Looking back and reading my diary, I learned a number of insights about my youthful self.

1. Like most other airmen flying in jets, I was an arrogant, cocky and spirited young man.

2. The end of day entries in my diary were almost exclusively in the present tense. Like many soldiers, I lived in the present, focused in the place and time I was experiencing. I wasn't interested in objectively standing back to take pictures of the extraordinary scenes I witnessed. I regret not capturing those Kodak moments.

3. At first, the Labrador countryside seemed desolate. Over time, viewed from my airborne perch, the countryside became beautiful.

4. The scope and variety of my reading interests back then surprised me. Fortunately, the base library was well stocked. The choices of the philosophical, spiritual and self-help passages I copied in my diary revealed my youthful reactions to the challenges confronting me. I also found the entries about the human behavior around me interesting.

5. Fighting boredom had to be much easier for me and other flight officers since we had the excitement of flying, often under challenging conditions. Our ground enlisted support airmen and officers didn't have the same opportunities for escaping Goose as our flight crews. For example, on several occasions during my year of remote duty, I escaped Goose when I flew overnight missions to Newfoundland. I had the opportunity for a three week break when I was assigned to help ferry an aircraft to the Lockheed plant in California. In the middle of the year I had leave time to return to the States. Courtesy of the Base Commander's invitation, my new bride was able to visit Goose for several weeks.

The greatest legacy from writing *Black Watch Diary* came from my oldest daughter, Thiery, who was conceived during her mother Naunie's visit to Goose's Degink "hotel": "Hi Dad, thanks for sending the copy to me to read. I enjoyed it.

Black Watch Diary

It made me feel and think many things. It really gave me a sense of what it must've been like at Goose – exciting, scary, primitive (at least by today's standards) isolating, comradeship and fun, COLDddddd, learning and adventure – all when you were just a couple years older than Andrew (son). It seems some tough things were thrown your way then – being separated such a distance from your new love so quickly, Faircloth being the only one excited about your coming marriage on Mom's side (yours too?), living in such a harsh, experimental environment, so many flight accidents, especially the fatal ones, but missing Bob Hope on New Years Day? Unforgiveable – Uncle Sam owes you. Its lovely to get such a rare peek into my father's world. Love you, Thiery."

Al Kramer's wife, Barbara was kind enough to share with me the extraordinary events of Al's military and civilian life which are summarized here. After Goose Air Base, Al Kramer, pilot, was assigned to Paine Field, Everett, Washington. Six weeks later he was transferred to the 460th Fighter Interceptor Squadron to continue flying F-89's.

Under "Operation Boot Strap," Al was assigned to the University of Washington to earn a mechanical engineering degree. While attending classes there he was a flight instructor in C-47's. Next, at McClellan Air Force Base, California in depot engineering, he received orders to fly C-54's based in Vietnam flying R&R (rest and relaxation) flights from Tan Son Nhat to Japan, Hong Kong, and Bangkok.

Barbara, Al's wife, in 1964 got a visa to visit Vietnam. During a four month stay, she had many fascinating experiences that deserve to be told in a memoir recounting the family's life in world-wide Air Force assignments that continued to Maguire AFB, New Jersey. Here, Al flew Lockheed C-130 Transports to carry cargo and personnel to world wide points. Three years later Al was in Spain with the 67th Air Rescue and Recovery Squadron, and Barbara got the opportunity to expand her college major in Spanish. Al really liked this duty. He was deployed to Mauritius on alert for a space shot. On one mission his crew dropped PJ's (Para Jumpers) who provided emergency medical aid to a Russian sailor aboard ship in the Atlantic Ocean.

Two years later, the Kramers were stationed in Woodbridge, England. Special treatment by the British government was accorded the 67th officers and their wives in appreciation for their work as the group rescued several British airmen in the jungles of Vietnam.

Josh Batchelder

After enjoying the family trips to the continent during Al's leave time, the Air Force sent Al to the Ogden, Utah Logistics Center. Horseback riding in the great northwest by all the family ended when "out of the blue" Al got orders to travel to Eielson AFB, Alaska where 50 degrees below zero temperatures could last a week. During off times, Al enjoyed taking his family flying in the base Cessna C-172 to nearby lakes to practice water landings. Soon Al taught his daughter, Valerie to fly and she later became a flight instructor. Subsequently, she married a professor at the University of Alaska where they now reside.

Four years of duty working and enjoying the great outdoors of frontier Alaska came to an end when the Air Force called Al back to the lower 48 at Holloman AFB, New Mexico. Two years later Al retired from the Air Force and he and Barbara returned to their roots in Augusta, Kansas. Al worked for Boeing and then Beechcraft retiring finally at age 65. In recent years Al has been working to become ambulatory again after suffering Parkinson's disease. Barbara, his very special companion and helper, drives him where he needs to go and continues her interest in crafts and teaching ceramics, jewelry design, stained glass and computer graphics. *We all await the memoir of this extraordinary Air Force family - JB*

The following is an excerpt from the obituary of Colonel Robert E. Fristch, USAF, Retired:

"Robert E. Fritsch, retired Colonel age 77, died peacefully Saturday, January 27, 2007. Bob was most proud of his military career as a veteran of the United States Air Force and Wisconsin Air National Guard as a Radar Observer. He loved to refer to himself as 'Old RO' and flew in F-94 and F-89 jet fighters. Bob's true passion was to teach. He constantly sought to challenge and expand people's knowledge. It was through teaching that Bob was able to touch and influence so many people in his life. He was a devoted family man, a master of literature, a great story teller, loved traveling, and photography. Last but not least, he was an avid Green Bay Packer football fan and we enjoyed many stories about his brother, Ted Fritsch, a Green Bay Packer Hall of Fame player during the 1940's."

"What is death? A step thru a dark doorway, now the real adventure begins. Weep no tears for me for I have lived. Let my epitaph read 'He loved and was loved' and that's enough for one lifetime."
 –R.E. Fritsch 2006

Black Watch Diary

Fergus Fay passed away June 17, 2008. The following is excerpted from his obituary:

"Ferg Fay of Roseburg, Oregon, 'flew' home to be with the Lord on Tuesday, June 17th, 2008. Fergus soloed after 4.5 hours of instruction at the age of sixteen and continued to fly until May 2008. He spent most of WWII flying AT-6s, P-40s, P-51s, and P-38s. There were very few planes that he didn't get to fly at least once."

"After being 'needed' at the Pentagon in Washington, D.C., he begged to return to the cockpit as a jet fighter in 1953. There he joyfully flew P-80s, T-33s, and the F-94 all weather fighers. He commanded a squadron in Portland, Oregon and Goose Bay, Labrador before they put him back in a classroom to inspire and teach young cadets. After retiring from the Air Force, Fergus was quickly hired by North American Aviation and worked on projects such as the F-100, B-70, B-1B, and the Space Shuttle. After 28 years with the company, he watched as the Space Shuttle Atlantis was launched, then promptly retired. He spent the next two years working full time on the famous Voyager: 'Round the World, Non Stop, Non Refueling.' This project with Bert Rutan, Dick Rutan, Jeana Yeager, and many others proved to be his most personally rewarding endeavor."

See pages 24-28 for a detailed account of the history of the Scramble Inn written by Al Perry, 59th Fighter Interceptor Squadron, Goose Bay, Labrador 1953-54. The following narrative, also written by Al Perry, descibes the continuing leagcy of the Scramble Inn.

Scramble Inn - Postmortem

Fast forward to circa 1970, Washington, D.C. Now a long time civilian, Al Perry and his wife Joy (post Air Force bride) were at a cocktail party that included several career Air Force officers. Speaking with two fighter type colonels, Al commented, "I was a flyer in the Air Force during the Korean era. Where have you two been based during your careers?"

One of the colonels replied, "Oh, places like Goose Bay, Labrador." Enjoying the moment, Al asked, "is The Scramble Inn still there?" Totally surprised the colonel responded, "It sure is and has become a serious BOQ Mess with full facilities."

"How do you know about it, Al?" He asked.

"Well, you may be surprised to know that it was built by our era 59th Fighter Squadron!" The colonel mused, "Not possible, Al. No one could have built that legend, it just happened."

Josh Batchelder

Al then proceeded to describe in detail the design of The Scramble Inn, particularly the design of the bar which he had created, but the look on the colonel's face made it clear that time had fostered a squadron legend and they did not want it spoiled by mortality. So, wistfully, Al conceded, "Yes colonel, I guess you're right...The Scramble Inn just happened."

The moral of this story is that it is true,
"Esprit de Corps" breeds legends, so let us enjoy one of ours!

Glossary

Radio communications commonly used terms for brevity and clarity in air to ground radio talk.

AB – Afterburner.

ANGELS - Altitude in thousands of feet.

APPLEJACK – The highest state of readiness during an air defense exercise.

BANDIT – Enemy aircraft (real).

BIG BANG – A nuclear explosion.

BOGEY – Enemy aircraft (simulated).

BUSTER – Use military power (full throttle without afterburner).

CHICKS – Friendly fighters.

CONTACT – I have the bogey on my radar scope.

FIVE BY – Your transmission is loud and clear.

GATE – Full power with afterburner.

HOME PLATE – The base where we were planning to land.

JUDY – I am taking over the intercept.

LEMON JUICE – The second highest state of readiness during an air defense exercise.

Josh Batchelder

M.A. – Mission Accomplished.

M.I. – Missed Intercept.

NO JOY – I have no radar or visual contact with the bogey.

OVER – I am done with my transmission, and listening for your reply.

PIGEONS – The heading and distance to Home Plate or some other base.

PORT – Left turn or left side.

ROGER – I heard and understood your transmission.

RTB – Return to base.

SPLASH – The bandit is destroyed.

STARBOARD - Turn right, or rightside

Black Watch Diary

International Phonetic Alphabet*

A	Alpha		N	November
B	Beta		O	Oboe
C	Cocoa		P	Papa
D	Delta		Q	Quebec
E	Echo		R	Romeo
F	Foxtrot		S	Sierra
G	Golf		T	Tango
H	Hotel		U	Uniform
I	India		V	Victor
J	Juliet		W	Whiskey
K	Kilo		X	X-Ray
L	Lima		Y	Yankee
M	Metro		Z	Zulu

*Note: The designations listed above were used during the time period of this diary. The current International Phonetic Alphabet was made by international agreement and adopted in 1957. *Beta, Cocoa, Metro,* and *Oboe* were replaced by *Bravo, Charlie, Mike,* and *Oscar.*

Josh Batchelder

Notes

[1] The hangar doors were designed to kick out, and up, to clear away snow accumulation.

[2] http://canadanorthoutfitting.bigbluesky.ca/hebron.htm

[3] http://explorenewfoundlandandlabador.com

[4] http://happyvalley-goosebay.com/climaticdata.htm (1951-1980). Rex Winchell, Allison Engines Technical Representative, reported that "Goose Airbase had over 200 inches (16ft.) of snowfall between 1 January and 17 June, 1954." The pictures he sent me support this account as did the packed snow I saw upon my spring 1954 arrival.

[5] In Bob Russell's book, *Touching the Face of God*, Huntington House Publishers (1992), he wrote his first impression on the approach to landing at Goose. See the Epilogue for Bob's extraordinary life after Goose.

[6] 59th Fighter squadron history: http://59thfis.org/history.htm

[7] Fighter squadron airmen are a notoriously spirited and cohesive group. The more conservative separate "ground pounder" officers on base along with the base HQ "weenies" were regularly offended by the songs, drinking, "uninhibited" dancing and talk of the 59th flyboys.

[8] Don Rogers described the "creative resourcefulness" of his squadron mates; "The ceiling plumbing under the BOQ was dramatically screened by a superb orange and white parachute donated as condemned property by the Base Supply Officer and put in place by Lee Grude and his happy crew of volunteers.

"But the crown jewel of the decor was the ceiling light over the bar. It was the canopy of an F-94 which had been sand blasted on the inside and sprayed with soft blue paint. It was spectacular! As to its source, my informant suffered from bouts of senility as to how the squadron came by it. How to turn the ugly cement basement walls and floors into pleasant colors? Ken Lengfield and his crew prayed for divine intervention for the Sherwin Williams trash pile fairy, and from old buckets of yellow, green, purple, red and blue, they concocted a disco hue and 'voila,' perfection!"

[9] Indian Dice, How to Play-two or more players five dice - http://www.ehow.com/how_2080845_play-indian-dice.html

[10] Fictitious

[11] Fictitious

[12] http://pinetreeline.org/boundary/canada.html

[13] Thule history: http://www.whoi.edu/beaufortgyre/hostiry/history_dew.html

[14] Atmospheric Disturbances: http://en.wikipedia.org/wiki/Radio_propagation

[15] www.ourlabrador.ca/member

[16] http://www.ourlabrador.ca/member.php?id=4

[17] Dave White's recall about Mac's rescue feat, "as I remember the story, after he shot his way out, with the plane on fire, Mac released the canopy but it only came up a few inches and he had to muscle it open far enough for Bill to get out. He burned his hands in the process and I remember the bandages on them for some time afterward. Later he was awarded a medal (I forgot which one) for heroism."

[18] At the Air Force Museum, Dayton, Ohio, there is a high speed experimental saucer-shaped vehicle. These vehicles were tested in our northern region.

[19] St. John's Newfoundland Paper. www.UFO.com/on this day/February10

[20] Hurricane Hazel: http://www.hurricanehazel.ca/

[21] On head-on approaches, there is limited observable surface for an aircraft's radar to reflect waves; broadside has much more reflecting surface.

[22] The U.S. Air Force Museum at Dayton, Ohio has an experimental flying saucer craft.

[23] The P-61 was the first operational all-weather fighter-interceptor. Northrop Aviation built this twin engine aircraft during WWII. Its top speed was 425 mph. Its armament was four twenty mm cannons, plus four fifty calibre machine guns. The radar antenna was in the

nose. It had a crew of three: Pilot, Radar Operator, and Gunner. D-Day, June 6, 1944, it first entered combat. Black Widows destroyed 127 enemy aircraft and 18 German Buzz Bombers (Air & Space Museum, Chantilly, Virginia has a P-61 on display).

[24] He believed that a large fleet of B-47 Bombers was the intimidating strategy to prevent war. (Air & Space Museum theme).

[25] The youthful enthusiasm of four successful active-air intercepts is like completing four touchdown passes - a celebration?

[26] The next thirty-three years Dave flew for TWA, retiring as a captain on B-747s.

[27] Air Force joke, in-the-air equipment - radios, aircraft systems present problems which can be due to atmospheric or other reasons. For expample on the F89D we experienced a UHF radio failure at high altitude (about 30,000 feet). At lower altitude it corrected itself. We discovered it was the very cold temperature contraction of a metal cable connection at extreme temperatures.

[28] An explosive shell fires to shoot the seat up, out and away from the cockpit.

[29] Ferrying an F-94B to Ontario Airport, California took an unusual amount of time. The short range operating capability of about six hundred miles required many refueling stops. Cross country flights also meant allowing enough fuel in reserve to fly to an alternate airfield if weather or runway conditions forced closing (accident on runway, iced conditions, maintenance fixes, etc.). Adverse wind conditions for example, prevailing strong winds from the west at altitude when making westward flights like jet streams at altitude, would mean much slower ground speed and longer flight times. When F-89D Scorpions arrived they more than doubled the range and time we could remain airborne.

[30] FZ@# It I Got My Orders

Black Watch Diary

59th Squadron Stations*

Mitchel Field, New York 15 Jan. 1941
(Operated from Tumbell Field, Groton, CT. 8-14 Dec. 41)
Glen L. Martin Airport, Baltimore, MD. 15 Dec. 41
(Operated from Millville, NJ April - 9 May 42)
Municipal Airport, Philidelphia, PA 10 May-12 Oct. 42
(Operated from Paine Field, Wash. 21 May-Jun 42)
Port Lyautey, French Morocco 10 Nov 42
Cases Airdrome, Casablance, French Morocco 15 Nov 42
Thelepte, Tunisia 8 Jan 43
Youds-les-Bains, Algeria 10 Feb 43
Telergma, Algeria 12 Feb 43
Berteaux, Algeria 2 Mar 43 (operated from Sbeitla, Tunisia 20 Mar-12 Apr 43)
Edda Ksour, Tunisis 12 Apr 43
Menzel Temine, Tunisia 15 May 43
Sousse, Tunisia 9 Jun 43
Pantelleria, Tunisia 16 Jun 43
Licata, Sicily 16 Jul 43
Milazzo, Sicily 2 Sept 43
Paestum, Italy 13 Sept 43
Santa Maria Capua, Italy 18 Nov 43
Cercola, Italy 1 Jan-5Feb 44
Karachi, India 10 Feb 44
Fungwanshum, China 19 Mar 44
Moran, India 5 Sept 44
Monhanbari, India 18 Oct 44
Nagaghuli, India 21 Nov 44
Dudkhundia, India 15 May-nov 45
Camp Shanks, NY 7-8 Dec 45
Neubiberg, Germany 20 Aug 46
Bad Kissingen, Germany 5 Jul-25 Aug 47
Andrews Field, MD 28 Aug 47
Roswell Army Air Field, NM (later Walker AFB) 16 Sept 47
Otis AFB, MA 16 Nov 48-28 Oct 52
Goose Bay (later Goose AB), Labrador 28 Oct 52-1 Jan 67
(operated detachment out of Thule, Greenland Sept. 52-Aug/Sept 53)

Josh Batchelder

Bergstron AFB, TX 1-2 Jan 67
Kingsley Field, OR 30 Sept 68-17 Dec 69
Eglin AFB, FL 1 Sept. 70-15 Apr 99
Reactivated to current service at Nellis AFB, NV testing Lockheed F-22

Squadron Aircraft

P-39, 1941-42
P-40, 1942-44
P-47, 1944-45
P-38, 1945
P-51 (later F-51) 1946-49
F-84, 1948-50
F-86, 1950-51
F-94B, 1951-55
F-89D & J, 1954-60
F-102, 1960-66
F-101, 1968-69
F-4E, 1974-79
F-15, 1979-99

Squadron Commanders

Major Mark E. Hubbard, Nov 42
Capt. J. O. Crowder, 8 May 43
Major Mark E. Hubbard, 12 Mar 43
Capt. Charles H. Duncan, 4 May 43
Capt. Donald A. Halliday, 3 Sept 43
Major Blanchard K. Watts, 21 Jan 44
Capt. Walter L. Moore, Jr., 2 Feb 44
Capt. Richard K. Turner, 2 mar 45
Capt. Frank A. Duncan, 1 Apr 45
Capt. Charles R. Langdon, 20 Apr 45
Capt. John W. Sogneir, 23 may 45
Capt. Edward R. Tyler, 12 Jun 45

Black Watch Diary

Capt. Howard Schulte, 26 Aug 45
Major Chester L. Can Etten, 20 Aug 46-Mar 47
Major Frank Q. O'Conner, 7 Nov 47
Lt. Col. Albert A. Cory, 10 May 48
Major Jarold J. Quandt, 2 Jun 48
Lt. Col. Woodrow W. Karges, 27 Jul 48
Major Jack C. West, 4 Mar 49
Lt. Col. Oscar R. Coen, 17 Jan 50
Lt. Col. Robert Dow, Dec 51-Oct 53
Major Morris F. Wilson, Aug 51
Lt. Col. Robert Dow, Dec 51-Oct 53
Lt. Col. Fergus C. Fay, Oct. 1953
Major Voy Winders, 1954
Major Francis R. Davison, July 1954
Major Victor G. Prarat, 10 January 1955
Lt. Colonel Victor E. Walton, 10 February 1955
Lt. Colonel William A. Shomo, 4 May 1955
Lt. Col. Leonard F. Koehler, 57
Lt. Col. Frank R. Jones, 1 Apr 61
Col. Edward R. Haydon, 8 Jan 63
Col. William J. Murphy, Jr., 1 Ju. 65
Major Robert J. Skinner, 15 Jun 66
Col. Dale L. Flowers, 29 Jun 66
Lt. Col. William Savidge, 30 Sept 68
Lt. Col. Ronald J. Layton, 30 Jun 69-unk.
Lt. Col. Peter K. Nicolos, 1 Jul 73-Jul 75
Lt. Col. Robert D. Rasmussen, 1 Jul 75-1 Apr 77
Lt. Col. John P. Heffernan, 1 Apr 77-22 Mar 79
Lt. Col. Jerry Cox, 23 Mar 79-13 Mar 81
Lt. Col. John R. Lippolt, 13 Mar 81-31 Jul 81
Lt. Col. Rudolph U. Zuberbuhler, 31 Jul 81 1 Jun 83
Lt. Col. William K. Matthews, 1 Jun 83-29 May 85
Lt. Col. James D. Woodall, 29 May 85-29 May 87
Lt. Col. Stevan G. Wilson, 29 May 87-20 Jan 89
Lt. Col. Michael E. Fain, 20 Jan-89-19 Feb 91
Lt. Col. James H. Davis, 19 Feb 91-6 Jul 92
Lt. Col. James G. Boehm, 6 Jul 92-8 Jul 94
Lt. Col. Michael J. Losor, 8 Jul 94-8 Jul 95

Josh Batchelder

Lt. Col. Mark A. Morris, 8 Jul 95-1 may 97
Lt. Col. Thomas A. McCarthy, 1 May 97 - unk.

In Memorium
Those who served during the author's time at Goose Bay

1953-1954

Robert B. Barton, Bob Booth, Bob Besett, Dean R. Blincow, James Clark, William H. Donahue, David Goodnough, Louis Hilstad, Fred R. Hinckley, Murray E. Hird, Ronald L. Jesiorkowski, David N. Lerly, John N. Savage, Louis I. Schreiner, James S. Thomas and Voy A. Winders.

1954-1955

Robert E. Baker, Rovert A. Brims, Robert L. Canup, Robert R. Craner, Belak A. Culpepper, Cecil F. Daniel, John T. Dennington, Thomas D. Dugosh, Hans A. Einstein, James R. Fuller, Philip E. Gereau, Edwin H. Golbertson, Jerome J. Gillies, John D. Harrington, Harlen J. King, John J. McGee, Jr., Donald E. Morrison, Gilbert S. Palmer, Victor, H. Prarat, Miles E. Standish, Wilford H. Taylor, Victor E. Walton and Robert J. Wells.

1955-1956

Phillip E. Crawford, Robert G. Ewals, William E. Fagan, Charles R. Hale, Sr., Claude F. Hanson, James A. Hillis, John R. Keeton, Bruce K. Leford, Richard J. Simpson, Robert G. Smith, Richard W. Smithson, Richard D. Stitt, Robert J. Stone and William A. Shomo.

*Information courtesy of Don Rogers, Fergie Ferguson, Robert Fritsch, and Thomas Woit.

About The Author

A retired U.S. Air Force Lt. Colonel, Josh Batchelder has logged over 5,000 hours of flying time, earning three different sets of silver wings—first as a Radar Observer (RO), flying in All-Weather Jet Fighter-Interceptors (Lockheed Starfire F-94Bs & Cs, then in Northrop F-89D Scorpions) for Air Defense squadrons based in Labrador, Canada, Washington State, Massachusetts, and New Hampshire. While completing a degree in Social and Personality Psychology at Harvard, he flew for the Massachusetts and New Hampshire Air National Guard units. More training and a second set of wings as an Air Navigator prepared him to fly world-wide missions for ten years, including several to Vietnam, with the 116th Military Airlift Wing of the Georgia Air National Guard (C-97 & C-124 transports). He became Wing Navigator. Completing 30 years of Air Force duty, his last assignment in the active Air Reserve was as a Reserve Assistance Officer (Liaison) to the Georgia Wing of the Civil Air Patrol (CAP). He conducted Flight Clinics and supported Aerospace Education programs for programs at the Universities of Georgia and Tennessee. Following active service, he became a volunteer in the Georgia CAP, earning his third set of wings as an instrument-rated private pilot, and flew search and rescue missions while serving as an Aerospace Education Officer. Josh is a member of the Atlanta chapter of the Silver Wings Fraternity.

In civilian life, Josh became a multi-year Million Dollar Round Table (MDRT) producer and Investment Advisor associated with Resource Horizons Group, LLC Broker/Dealer, Marietta, Georgia. In 1976, he completed training and was certified as a graphoanalyst (handwriting analyst). For four major cruise lines, he entertained onboard audiences with talks and demonstrations. This led to publication of his first book, *Handwriting Reveals You* (2003), and three years later to publishing of *Personality Profiling in 90 Seconds: A 15-Point Guide for Quick Handwriting Analysis.*

He continues to present programs for commercial, private, and civic groups. Visit his website, *www.quickprofiling.com*, for information on how to purchase either of the books or schedule an informative and entertaining program.

Josh is father to four adult children and seven grandchildren, plus the four children and five grandchildren he acquired some ten years ago, upon his marriage to Betty Ann Sage — the "wise one." Betty Ann and Josh live in Atlanta as co-owners of one remaining "child" who has *them* on a leash—Kelly, a miniature Schnauzer.